Beyond Our Wildest Dreams

A History of
Overeaters Anonymous
as Seen by a Cofounder

OVEREATERS ANONYMOUS®

ISBN 1-889681-00-8
Library of Congress Catalog Card No.: 96-70336

Overeaters Anonymous, Inc.
6075 Zenith Court NE
Rio Rancho, New Mexico 87124-6424 USA
Mail Address: P.O. Box 44020
Rio Rancho, NM 87174-4020 USA
1-505-891-2664

Printed in the United States of America.
Imprimido en los Estados Unidos.

A Note to the Reader:

In order to preserve the flavor and accuracy of quoted material and excerpts, we have retained the punctuation, capitalization and style that were present in the original sources. These occasionally differ from the overall text of the book.

Disclaimer

To those who have provided assistance in preparing and providing approval of this book, we thank you. To those who were involved in some of the events depicted in this book, but who are not mentioned, we apologize. The names or locations of some individuals, whom we could not find or were unable to contact, have been modified. And to those who have so graciously participated and given of themselves in the history of OA, but are no longer with us: Your actions are now recorded, and your memories will always remain with us.

Contents

". . . We are all together now, reaching out our hands
for power and strength greater than ours, and as we
join hands, we find love and understanding beyond
our wildest dreams."

from *I Put My Hand In Yours*
by Rozanne S.

Put Your Hand in Mine . . .

. . . and explore with me OA's earliest years (and some recent ones as well). Learn what we were like, what happened, what we're like now and what we dream for the future.

It's been a memorable adventure. Often hectic, sometimes upsetting, always soul-satisfying, the birth and development of Overeaters Anonymous has been a miracle in the making.

Writing this story has been like going through the attic of my mind. Memories long-forgotten have been dusted off. Many original members were interviewed, old tapes listened to while voices from the past drifted through my life once more.

Studying thousands of transcript pages from Conference, trustee and committee meetings clarified my recollections. Hundreds of letters dating from early responses to the 1960 Paul Coates TV interview reflected our growing pains. Business correspondence beginning with the first 1962 Board of Trustees recalled our struggles to establish a firm foundation.

Original meeting formats, directories and mailings, decades-old *OA Bulletins* and *OA Lifelines* and archival materials of all kinds helped to create an accurate record of the astonishing growth of Overeaters Anonymous.

Now it's your turn to walk the path taken by the earliest OA members. Experience the triumphs and troubles, the struggles and sharing, the courage and commitment.

This is *our* Fellowship and *our* history. Enjoy!

Rozanne S.
Cofounder, Overeaters Anonymous

Prelude
November, 1958

THE best stories are those which begin simply, unexpectedly. This is just such a story.

It was ten o'clock one chilly November night in West Los Angeles, California. Marvin and I had been married barely three years. My first daughter, Debbie, was only twenty months old, and I'd just had another baby girl, Julie, eight months earlier. That night the house was quiet; my husband and babies were asleep. It was time for my late-night routine of TV watching and eating.

"Paul Coates' Confidential File should be interesting," I mused. He was a TV interviewer and nationally-syndicated journalist, and his subjects were always thought-provoking. Flipping the dial, I settled in to binge and watch. Twenty-nine years old, 5'2" tall and 152 pounds, I spent every night until bedtime filling my inner emptiness with excess food.

"Tonight," Paul Coates began, "we're going to hear from a member of a new group called Gamblers Anonymous." As the interview progressed, I became increasingly fascinated. "Why doesn't that man turn around?" I wondered. "Why does he keep his back to the camera?" Momentarily forgetting to eat, I listened to a discussion of a subject and concepts totally foreign to my experience. No matter—my husband had a friend who was a compulsive gambler, and with my mouth full of food, I said to myself, "This thing would be just great for him." My dormant drive as a world-saver was about to be awakened.

The next morning I called the local GA office for the meeting place and address. "It's at the old Mayflower Hotel in downtown Los Angeles," the friendly phone voice reassured me. Marshalling our forces of persuasion, Marvin and I coaxed his friend to join us at a GA meeting.

As long as I live, I will never forget that night. We were in a meeting hall with about twenty-five men and a sprinkling of wives. Sitting in the back of that room, my big black coat clutched around me, I heard men talk about lives of lying and cheating, stealing and hiding. "Now," they assured us, "we no longer have to live that way."

I sat there transfixed; they seemed to be speaking directly to me. "I'm just like that," I said to myself. "The only difference is that I overeat instead of gamble." Overwhelmed, I thought, "I'm not alone anymore."

That night I learned that I wasn't wicked or sinful; I was sick. I had an illness, which I was later to call compulsive overeating. It was all a revelation to me, and when I walked out of the meeting room that night, my life changed forever.

I wanted to talk to other overeaters, so I looked in the phone book for TOPS, the only well-known weight-loss organization available at that time. TOPS wasn't listed, so I tried to find Fatties Anonymous. Somewhere I'd heard about that, too. I couldn't find either one. Terrified, I didn't know where to turn. Where could I go? What should I do?

I clung to my diet for the next three weeks, then gave in and went back to my old ways. I continued to overeat for another year. Then, in late 1959, weighing 152 pounds and wearing a size eighteen, I hit a plateau. For awhile it seemed that I could eat as much as I wanted and still not gain weight. Food was hidden everywhere around my house. I hated myself and was afraid of life; I felt totally worthless. Over and over I tried to exert my willpower, but I just couldn't do it alone.

Helpless and hopeless, I didn't know that I needed other people for support and a life-changing program for recovery.

Interlude
December, 1959

IT was November, 1959, exactly a year since our visit to Gamblers Anonymous. New neighbors had just moved in down the block. The woman, Jo S., weighed over two hundred pounds, and I'd never seen anyone who looked like her. She carried her excess weight all in front, and I said to myself, "I'll never look like that. I'll never let myself weigh that much." Those are famous last words for an overeater!

Holiday time was coming, and in early December my three-year-old Debbie and I flew to White Sands, New Mexico, for a visit with my brother, Chuck, and his family. My parents flew in from Chicago to join us, and with all the excitement and my parents' presence, many of my childhood memories were awakened.

Since my sister-in-law, Syd, was a wonderful cook, food was everywhere all the time. It was all too much for me, and the only way I could cope with my unrecognized feelings was to eat and eat.

Returning home to Los Angeles, I headed straight for the scale. What a shock—I had gained nine pounds in a week and a half! Now weighing 161 pounds, I wore a size twenty. I'd never weighed that much, never been that fat. I was only thirty years old. Despairing and hopeless, I felt my world was crumbling around me. Years of conventional psychotherapy hadn't stemmed my overeating; doctors and diets hadn't helped either.

Only two months earlier I'd scoffed at my new neighbor, Jo, and now I knew I'd look like her in almost no time at all. What could I do next?

Frantic and desperate, I remembered that night at Gamblers Anonymous. I told my husband, "Marvin, I can't find any group, so I'm going back to Gamblers Anonymous to see if it's the same as I remember." My supportive husband encouraged me, and off I went to find hope and a new life.

Returning to GA, I found it a year stronger and more inspiring. By late 1959 the group was two and a half years old; several of the men I'd heard before were still there. Their stories were even more encouraging; many had not made a bet since GA's first meeting. Recovery was everywhere, and they welcomed me warmly.

Listening to the men talk, I knew that this was what I needed, except that it was the wrong compulsion. Could I re-create that sense of belonging for myself and others like me? The more I thought about it, the more I was sure that a group like Gamblers Anonymous would work for compulsive overeaters like me. Since I couldn't find anything, I would have to start it myself.

After the meeting I approached Jim W., the founder of Gamblers Anonymous. It must have been quite a sight—a 5'2", overweight young woman staring up into the face of 6'2", skinny middle-aged man.

Trembling, I asked, "Jim, do you think an organization like yours could work for compulsive overeaters like me?"

He smiled down at me gently. "I don't see why not. I was in Alcoholics Anonymous before I ever started GA. Tell me what you have in mind."

I took a breath and began to describe it all—my bingeing and despair, my visit to GA the year before and its impact upon me, my idea of an organization for myself and others like me.

"Rozanne," he asked, "are you talking about starting a local group or a few groups in the city?"

"Oh, no," I shook my head vehemently. "I know that

someday my organization will be as big as AA or bigger, and it will be all around the world."

Someone else might have laughed at my grandiose visions, but not Jim. "You can do it," he urged me. "I did it, and GA is really growing. I'll help you."

There it was—a hand outstretched to steady me as I stumbled along! It was my first experience with the Twelfth Step, the first time anyone had offered to help me with no thought of return.

Jim wasn't a compulsive overeater, but his understanding and love for overeaters never faltered. From that night on he offered encouragement, support and guidance as I struggled to develop our infant Fellowship.

With my usual self-willed zeal, I sailed into saving the world. Approaching some of the GA wives about my new weight-loss idea, I was soundly rebuffed. Next I tried the overweight women at my daughter's nursery school. I was certain they would welcome my help in losing weight. Their rejection was swift and unexpected. I was confused. Why didn't they want my help? "I see you have the same weight problem I do," I would tell them. "Listen, I have this terrific idea for us to get thin." It didn't occur to me that I was calling them fat and that I was still fat myself. No wonder they didn't want to join me.

For the next few weeks I talked to fifteen or twenty women. Everyone had a reason, an excuse for not jumping on my bandwagon. Some had just lost weight, some were starting a new diet, some said they could manage with diet pills. It was very disheartening to me, because I heard myself in all these stories. All the things they said to me were things that I had said to myself. But by this time I knew that I didn't have it licked, that I had no willpower and that I was going nowhere without help.

During this period I began to consider a name for my new venture. I wanted a name like GA and AA, something with "Anonymous" in it.

I didn't like Fatties Anonymous. "What happens," I

thought, "when you become thin? Besides, who would want to come in and be labeled a fatty?"

"What do we all have in common?" I asked myself. "If the alcoholic is a compulsive over*drinker*, then we must be compulsive over*eaters*. We're not just normal overeaters; we overeat *compulsively*. But Compulsive Overeaters Anonymous is too long. It's difficult to say and awkward to remember. Overeaters Anonymous is better. It tells people exactly what we are, yet it won't discourage them from coming to us.

Was this the right name? How could I begin this venture? Who would join with me in the beginning?

One Sunday afternoon Marvin and I sat down to discuss the various options. I told him my ideas for the name. "What do you think of Overeaters Anonymous?" I asked. He smiled and nodded. "Sounds good to me."

"But how can I get this thing started?" I persisted.

"Well," he answered, "you know we both belong to that health club. Why don't you go down there? Maybe you can start something through them."

Marvin's input that afternoon was only the beginning. All through the years to follow, he would continue to offer support and encouragement to me in my personal and OA endeavors. His idea about the local health club seemed as good as any, so I tucked it away for future reference.

Christmas came and went. One crisp afternoon the last week in December, I was strolling my babies down the block. Suddenly, I spied my overweight, new neighbor across the street, starting out for a stroll with her baby. I didn't know her very well, but I remembered her name. "Hi, Jo," I called to her. "Wait for me."

She stopped, and I crossed to her side of the street. "Are you taking the kids to the park?" she asked as I fell into step beside her.

"Not today," I answered. We went a few steps farther and I began my pitch. "You know, I'm having a terrible time with my weight, and I see you have the same problem."

She met these words with stony silence, and instantly I

regretted my comment. I began to talk faster, to cover my blunder and show her I hadn't intended to be rude. It was obvious I needed to find another approach. Then I hit upon an idea.

"I can't walk too long," I said. "I have to go someplace important this afternoon."

"I see," she said curtly, and she changed the subject.

I scolded myself for ruining another opportunity to interest someone in the proposed organization. After the reactions of the other women I'd approached, I should have learned my lesson. Anything that even hinted at finger-pointing wouldn't do. Nobody wanted to hear nagging about weight loss.

I decided to try again, telling myself, "It's now or never!" As we approached my house, I said, "Jo, I've really got to hurry."

"What's the rush?" she inquired.

Frantically, I made up an excuse. "Well, I have to go to the health club to see about starting this group. But I know you wouldn't be interested."

"This group?" she asked. "What group?"

By this time we had reached my front door. I answered, "Well, I know you don't share this problem, but I'm a compulsive overeater and I'm having a terrible time."

Intrigued, she persisted. "What's the name of your group?"

I took a deep breath. "Overeaters Anonymous."

"You know," she offered, "I *would* be interested. I think I'd like to try it with you."

At that moment, the Fellowship of Overeaters Anonymous was born.

It Only
Takes Two . . .

few days later I went to see my family doctor. After a thorough examination, he discussed my weight problem with me. "Rozanne," he admonished, "you need to lose about fifty pounds, and I have just the thing for you. It's a pill called Dexedrine."

Remember, this was the beginning of the 1960s. Along with many others, I was naive regarding drugs, and I viewed my doctor as The Authority. Overstimulated as a result of the medicine, I stopped excessive eating, and for six months I had the cleanest house in Los Angeles! In that same period I went from 161 pounds to 120 pounds, and eventually to 110 pounds, a weight I maintained for several years. The medicine helped for the six months I took it, but my efforts to start OA were the most important factor in my dramatic weight loss.

Even before our first meeting my enthusiasm was boundless, and I wanted to return to GA for more information.

Jo had no knowledge of any Twelve-Step Fellowship. "Just wait," I coaxed her. "Come to a GA meeting with me and see what it's like."

"Absolutely not," she refused.

It took a lot of persuading on my part. "Come on, Jo," I persisted. "Besides, I know a GA wife who might be interested. Her name's Bernice. She's been going to meetings with her husband for over a year, and she'll be able to help us.

However, I don't have her phone number, so we'll have to go to a meeting to talk to her."

Reluctantly, Jo agreed to go. Once we got there, she was not greatly impressed with this little group of gamblers and their wives. She didn't feel the identification I had found, but at least she said she'd continue with me.

After the GA meeting we cornered Bernice and told her about the proposed Overeaters Anonymous. Assured that our organization was being formed, she decided to join with us and give it a try. In fact, Bernice offered her home for the first meeting. Since Jo and I had small children who would surely disrupt any gatherings at our houses, we readily agreed to meet at Bernice's home. We set our first meeting for the following Tuesday, January 12, 1960.

Within days, however, we all came down with the flu— my children, Jo's girls, Jo and her husband, Marvin and me. We spent our scheduled first meeting staggering from our beds only long enough to tend to sick babies. The founding meeting of Overeaters Anonymous would have to wait until the founders were over the flu.

Finally, the first OA meeting was held on the next Tuesday night, January 19, 1960, from eight o'clock to ten o'-clock in Bernice's Hollywood home.

One overeater talking to another. We didn't realize it that night, but the spiritual essence of all Twelve-Step groups was present among us. We shared a problem, we identified with one another, and we hoped for a common solution.

The three of us—Bernice, Jo and I—sat in Bernice's living room for two hours and talked about our weight problems and our attempts to diet. Actually, I tried to steer the conversation away from food and dieting as much as possible. I was a very analytical person and had been in therapy off and on for several years. I knew excess food was only a symptom of deeper problems.

The psychological catch phrase of the day was "inferiority complex," and we used that frequently as the cause of our overeating. In addition, I blamed my mother for many of my problems. It was to be many years of Twelve-Step work on myself before I could see that the causes lay within me.

Towards the end of that first meeting, I said to Jo and Bernice, "You know what? OA will be five thousand groups in fifteen years. You wait and see." As if that wasn't enough of a bombshell, I went on. "This meeting has been so great, I think I'll go to Jack Latham tomorrow." A Los Angeles TV news anchor, Latham had a small interview section at the end of his news programs. My vocational background had been in copywriting and advertising, so promotion came naturally to me.

I can still see the looks on their faces. "Jack Latham?" they exclaimed. "We haven't done anything yet." They made me promise not to seek any publicity for four months or they wouldn't come back to the second meeting.

I had nothing without Jo and Bernice, so I had no choice. Reluctantly, I agreed. "Okay, four months. We'll all lose weight, and then I'll go to Jack Latham." Impatient and self-willed, I couldn't wait to make OA grow.

As I think back, how could I have managed it all? I was only thirty years old, married just over four years. I was a young mother with two babies; my hard-working husband left early and came home at six o'clock for dinner each night.

OA became an integral part of my life from its beginning. I was obsessed with my vision, living and breathing it as I cared for my home and family.

The following Tuesday we met again, this time at Jo's house. With just three members, the meeting was very informal. We had no format yet, and none of us knew anything about working the Steps. I was faithfully counting my calories and weighing myself daily. Jo and I also talked between our weekly meetings. Frequently, we'd take our little girls to the park and discuss our problems and feelings while the children played in the sandbox.

Finally, I had hope. I'd found others who understood my struggles with food, kindred spirits to whom I could open my heart.

During those first couple of weeks, Jo and Bernice didn't share my enthusiasm about OA, but at least they were willing to discuss the things that made us want to overeat. For all of us, it was a relief to be able to talk about our feelings with someone who understood.

Prior to the first OA meeting, when Jo and I went to GA, I had bought both a slender GA pamphlet and the AA "Big Book." At Jim's urging, I read some of the AA book, including Chapter Five and the Twelve Steps. I found the AA book confusing but interesting. However, I scoffed at the folksy, Vermont writing style of AA's cofounder, Bill W. I felt that since he was a stockbroker and not a writer, he didn't know any better than to use that corny tone of voice. After all, I sniffed, I was a big-city girl, and I'd been a fashion copywriter for eight years. "I can do a better job on those Steps," I boasted to myself. I thought I knew it all.

With that attitude, I sat down at my typewriter one night with the AA and GA Steps in front of me and began to rewrite the Steps for OA.

I began by carefully reading GA's Steps. I hadn't studied AA's Steps, so until then I didn't realize that GA had slightly rewritten AA's Steps. GA's First Step talked about being powerless over gambling, and AA's Step One mentioned being powerless over alcohol. I simply could not accept the concept of powerlessness, but I could certainly admit that I was a compulsive overeater.

With that in mind, I took a deep breath and began typing my First Step. Because GA wrote about the action of gambling, it seemed only logical for me to write about the action of compulsive overeating rather than food. It was to be another year before I could admit I was "powerless over food."

Moving on to Steps Two and Three, I stopped. Although Judaism and its traditional values had been a major part of my upbringing, God and spirituality were rarely discussed at home while I was growing up.

Self-reliance and willpower were all-important in my family. Neither an atheist nor an agnostic, I was a skeptic, an intellectual and proud of it. How could I reconcile the Second and Third Steps with my parents' teachings? It seemed to me that Step Two could be softened by saying, "We admit that we need help—that a Power greater than ourselves can restore us to a normal way of thinking and living."

(Because I was primarily using GA's Steps as a guide, I didn't realize that they had removed AA's word "sanity" and replaced it with the phrase "normal way of thinking and living." This change was to cause tremendous arguments in OA from December, 1960, until our first National Conference in 1962.)

Step Three was a monumental stumbling block for me. I stared down at the paper, reading and rereading that Step. I could feel my back stiffening, my anger rising. I remember hitting my fist on the typewriter table in defiance. "Never!" I shouted to myself. "I am not so weak that I have to turn *my* will and *my* life over to the care of any God, whether I understand Him or not." I picked up my pen and put a big "X" through Step Three.

After this outburst, I paused. If OA was to be like AA and GA, I had to have Twelve Steps. People would expect twelve. I asked myself, "What would an intelligent, sophisticated person like me do instead of turning my will and my life over to God?" The answer seemed obvious: medical supervision for my dieting.

Doctors and diets seemed the next logical thing after admitting I was a compulsive overeater, so I moved Step Two down a notch and made it Step Three, and wrote my own brand new Second Step. Then I quickly deleted those offensive phrases about coming to believe and turning one's will and life over to God.

Next I came to Step Four. Because I'd studied psychology in college and had therapy in my teens, I understood the self-searching implied in this Step. But it seemed weak to me, so I decided to insist on action by adding the word "must." (Later I learned that Bill W. had taken the same tone in his first draft of AA's "Big Book," until his advisors reminded him

17

that alcoholics might not respond well to "musts." "Suggest," they said, would be more acceptable.)

The word "wrongs" in Step Five bothered me. "I haven't done anything wrong," I said to myself. "Difficulties" seemed a nice, safe substitution, easy to admit to someone else.

As soon as I'd done that, I began to worry that my Steps wouldn't be enough like AA's. After many attempts to get around it, I finally decided to mention God. Since I considered myself an intellectual, I felt the reference to a deity, buried here in the Seventh Step, would not be too offensive to people who thought as I did. However, I thought that simply asking God to remove our difficulties couldn't possibly work. I "corrected" it to make us responsible for removing our own shortcomings with God's help. In essence, I made God my helper instead of the other way around.

I didn't understand the necessity of using two Steps to take care of making amends to others; it didn't make sense to me. I felt I was a better writer than that, and shaking my head at those inefficient alcoholics and gamblers, I proceeded to combine Steps Eight and Nine. I also felt that "harmed" in Step Eight was the wrong word and that the only way we could hurt anyone was through direct actions, so I changed that part of my Step Eight as well.

AA's and GA's Step Ten was another psychological Step, in my opinion, so I just moved it into the place of the deleted Step Nine.

Now I stopped again. What could I use to replace the now-missing Step Ten? I carefully reread what I had written, and then I had what I thought was a bright idea. It's important to note that I was still a rebellious newcomer with no knowledge of what the original Twelve Steps were all about. Therefore, I still had the "diet mentality." I felt it was vital to have something about maintaining an eating plan in my new Twelve Steps, and the empty space for the former Step Ten seemed the perfect place. It's interesting to see that in spite of myself, I used the word "pray" in conjunction with lifelong maintenance of that eating plan.

By now I was beginning to feel distinctly uneasy about *not* having Steps that sounded like AA's. I was really afraid that people wouldn't think we were like AA, and after all, that was my main aim. Thus I just gave up and used Step Eleven in its original form, substituting the word "strength" for "power."

Step Twelve, however, was another matter. Spiritual awakening? Absolutely not! That phrase was totally foreign to my upbringing and experience. GA had removed those words from its Twelfth Step and slightly rewritten it, so I just copied their Step. I decided that if it was good enough for GA, it was all right for OA, as well.

It's interesting to see that I wrote most of the Steps in the present tense rather than the past tense, as the members of AA and GA had done. We had no past; I had not begun to work the Steps for myself, and neither had Jo or Bernice.

Here are the original Twelve Steps of Overeaters Anonymous, as I wrote them in January of 1960:

1. We admit that we are compulsive overeaters—that our lives have become unmanageable.
2. Before embarking on this program, we know that we must seek the aid of a physician of our own choosing, returning to him for regular checkups. We know that he, and only he, can advise us regarding our own calorie allotments and wisest nutritional program.
3. We admit that we need help—that a Power greater than ourselves can restore us to a normal way of thinking and living.
4. We must make a searching and fearless moral inventory of ourselves.
5. We have admitted to ourselves and to another human being the exact nature of our difficulties.
6. We are entirely ready to have these defects of character removed.
7. We humbly ask God (of our understanding) to help us remove our shortcomings.
8. We shall make a list of all persons we have hurt through our actions and willingly make amends to them.
9. We shall continue to take personal inventory, and when we are wrong, promptly admit it.

10. We shall set up a regular pattern of eating for ourselves, and this we pray we may maintain for the rest of our lives.
11. We must seek through prayer and meditation to improve our conscious contact with God as we understand Him, praying only for knowledge of His will for us and the strength to carry that out.
12. Having made an effort to practice these principles in all our affairs, we shall try to carry this message to other compulsive overeaters.

I was proud of the Twelve Steps as I had rewritten them. It never occurred to me that as a sick compulsive overeater and a newcomer who had never tried to work the program, I was not in the best position to judge AA's and GA's Twelve Steps, much less to change them. Sometime during the second meeting, I said to Jo and Bernice, "Girls, I really don't like the AA Twelve Steps at all, so I rewrote them. Tell me what you think." I read my new version to them.

Jo was an atheist, so she liked the rewrite of the Steps; perhaps Bernice was too polite to object. At that second meeting, untroubled by committees and delegates, I presented OA's first sheet of literature—the Twelve Steps rewritten as I wanted to work them—and it was approved by default, without a murmur. Never again in the history of OA would I get my way so easily.

By the third meeting, Jo's husband agreed to let us meet in his office on the second floor of a small office building on Pico Boulevard in Los Angeles. That third meeting almost ended Overeaters Anonymous. Bernice, Jo and I gathered and began our discussion. By this time I had lost fifteen pounds and was absolutely elated with my new figure. I started talking about how my diet was going and how I was losing weight.

At that moment there was silence. Then before we had a chance to continue, Bernice announced she was quitting the group. "My doctor says dieting is making me nervous," she said, "and I can't come anymore." With that, she got up and left.

Jo and I sat there looking at each other, stunned. I panicked. Was it over before it had started? "Dieting makes me nervous, too," I said. "I'm losing weight, but I can't do it by myself. What about you? Are you doing anything at all?"

For a moment, Jo didn't say anything. Then, unable to admit that she was still bingeing, she blurted out, "Are you nuts, Rozanne? This whole thing is crazy!"

I felt totally alone and miserable. I had pinned my hopes on Overeaters Anonymous, feeling certain that if I could have the kind of loving support the GA members gave each other, I could surely stop my compulsive overeating for good. Instead, I was alone, trying to diet. I knew that without help I would fail as I had always failed before. I started to cry. All my brash self-will and self-assurance had vanished. "Jo," I pleaded, "don't leave. I need help. I just can't do this alone. Please, please try it with me."

Later Jo would tell me she felt in that moment as if I'd thrown down the gauntlet and issued a challenge. "All right," she said at last. "I'll stay, and I'll stop cheating and do this thing with you."

True to her word, she did. From that moment on, Jo stopped overeating and began to lose weight rapidly. She and I worked closely together, followed our diets and held OA meetings from eight o'clock to ten o'clock every Tuesday night. At first there were just the two of us. During the meetings we sat in the big leather chairs in her husband's office and talked. We discussed our inferiority complexes, our mothers, our husbands and children and our frustrations that made us want to overeat.

We also talked between meetings, sometimes several times daily, calling each other on the phone to vent our feelings whenever we wanted to eat. We examined our anger, resentment, greed, envy (although we didn't use those terms) and feelings of inferiority.

We paid scant attention to the Steps, since neither of us had any idea about how to work them. It wasn't until several years later that I would do a Fourth-Step inventory. As flawed as our fledgling OA group was, however, we had one basic and vital ingredient—the fellowship of one overeater talking to another. We were giving each other understanding, encouragement and support. As months passed, it was working. We were staying out of the refrigerator and losing weight.

Jo and I went to one or two more GA meetings. I continued to talk with Jim W. on the phone, relying heavily on him for encouragement and advice. Knowing nothing about sponsors back then, I didn't realize that Jim was OA's first sponsor. He was a quiet man who helped me without ever telling me that things had to be done in a certain way. Everyone in OA, myself included, owes him an enormous debt of gratitude for the help he gave OA in our early days.

After a few weeks, Jim suggested that we visit an AA meeting. "Oh, I couldn't," I shot back. "They might be drunk and accost us."

Oh, the patience of Jim! "No, no," he laughed. "The drunks are in other places, but the sober people are in AA. Believe me, you'll be safe. You go to AA."

Jim knew I needed the experience, strength and hope I would find at AA meetings. He'd talked to me enough to know I was one of those examples of self-will run riot the "Big Book" talks about. I was starting my own game and making my own rules as I went along. I thought that with my new and improved Twelve Steps, OA would surely take off very quickly and outgrow AA in no time.

As the days went by, however, and Jo and I struggled along together, I decided perhaps Jim was right. I told Jo, "We're going to have to go to AA." Jo was even more horrified by this idea than I had been. Not only was she worried about being attacked by a drunk, she was mortified to think that someone might assume she was an alcoholic. But Jim had me convinced, and I insisted that the two of us were going to have to attend AA if we were ever to get our OA organization off the ground.

Despite her objections, Jo finally relented. Too proud to

admit it, I was scared too. We arrived one night at a large meeting filled with laughing and friendly people, and I found the same loving spirit I'd felt in GA. When it came time to pass the basket, Jo reached into her purse. The man next to her leaned over and whispered, "You don't have to put anything in if this is your first meeting."

Jo was utterly shattered. "Oh, Rozanne," she wailed later, "he thought I was one of them. He thought I was just another alkie."

Despite such fears, the AA meetings were very important to me and to OA. We desperately needed to learn what the recovering alcoholics could teach us about the Twelve-Step program. For the next ten years I went to open AA meetings. I was timid at first, but eventually I went to meetings once or twice a week. I encouraged other OA members to attend as well.

After OA's first year, local AA members would come to share their recovery at our little meetings, give us help over the telephone and welcome us as visitors at their open meetings. A few AA's even conducted study groups to help us learn more about the Twelve Steps and Twelve Traditions. We all felt so much gratitude for the love and unselfishness of those wonderful Los Angeles AA members. Without them, OA would not be as strong as it is today.

During that first year, Jim came to talk to us a few times, gently and patiently trying to explain the program to us despite our weakened Twelve Steps.

When I finally showed my rewritten version of the Steps to Jim, he just read them and said nothing. He must have been horrified at what I'd done to them, but he also knew I was a headstrong woman. He probably knew he'd have to bide his time before mentioning the subject of restoring the Steps.

However, during our earliest weeks, Tuesday nights often found Jo and me alone, sitting in those big leather chairs in her husband's office, talking about our inferiority complexes. After that fateful third meeting when Bernice left, Jo became very serious about her diet, and soon she was losing weight. Still taking my doctor's diet medication, I continued to lose weight very rapidly myself. Because I was weighing and measuring my food and eating only seven hundred to eight hundred calories a day, my excess fat was melting away. By March, 1960, I had lost 25 pounds. Instead of 161, I now weighed 136 pounds.

Jo was thinner, I was thinner, but it was a terrible struggle to get other women to show up for our meetings. Now and then two or three others would come, then leave again. What should we do?

Suddenly, in early April our luck changed! My husband's cousin, Mollie, had a neighbor, Barbara S., who'd gone to a "reducing farm," as we called the health spas then. Barbara had been home about two months when she started regaining the pounds she'd lost.

As Barbara later told me, "I was talking to Mollie, and I was in tears because here I was again, gaining weight."

"Oh, Barbara," Mollie exclaimed, "you should see Marvin's wife, Rozanne! She has some new group, and since January she's lost thirty pounds. Why don't you see what she's doing?"

Barbara remembers her reaction. "I hesitated," she explains, "and I didn't do it right away. It was only when I was at the end of my rope that I decided I'd call. And when I called you, you were so open to my coming down, so enthusiastic. I got the feeling when I called you, 'Here's someone who really understands.'"

During our phone conversation I discussed some of my own experience with the disease of compulsive overeating and shared my enthusiasm for the OA program. "Drive down to our meeting on Tuesday night," I encouraged her.

The following Tuesday, Barbara and a friend showed up at the meeting. Barbara would later tell me she was more than a little taken aback by the fact that I wasn't very heavy. She had no idea what I had looked like a few months before! "You were so understanding on the telephone," she protested. "How could someone who is slim understand someone like me who is heavy?"

"Rozanne has suffered, too," Jo assured her. We began to talk about all the ways we'd tried to lose weight. I told her about my dieting history, the years of therapy and the desperation that grew with each new failure and new top weight on the bathroom scales. Our sharing put Barbara at ease very quickly. She talked about her experience too. "I don't know what this meeting will do for me," she said, but she stayed and joined in. Later she would recall, "One of the important things was that we did enough talking about our problems at the meeting that I didn't need to talk to my friends, who never understood me anyway. I was very enthusiastic after that meeting, and I decided that there might be something to this."

Barbara became the third person to join us in OA and stick with us. She, too, quickly began to lose weight. She attended AA meetings with us, and she brought in other new people as well. She was very keen on building up OA because she felt strongly it was the only safe haven for compulsive overeaters. "People feel sorry for alcoholics and want to help them," she said, "but no one seems to have any sorrow for the overeater, other than being disgusted with our size. So we have to have compassion for ourselves. We have to get together for ourselves."

By early June, 1960, I decided to stop the diet pills. I had lost 40 pounds and now weighed 121. Jo was well on her way and would be 109 pounds by August. Barbara was losing rapidly, too. The program, such as it was, seemed to be working beautifully for the three of us.

But what about the others who drifted in and out? I was so frustrated. They just wouldn't get it, wouldn't stick to their diets, wouldn't lose weight. Unfortunately, we took their leaving as a personal rejection of us. We thought that they didn't like us, didn't love us. We worried that they felt we weren't with it at all, and that's why they were leaving.

One night Barbara, Jo and I discussed this and concluded that the problem lay with *them* and not with us, and that's why they were leaving. That discovery was an enormous relief to us. Still, as much as I insisted, those other women simply wouldn't share my enthusiasm. We knew we needed more members; I had to do something else!

All OA needed to really grow, I figured, was a little bit of publicity. My mind went back to the Paul Coates program, where I'd first heard about Gamblers Anonymous. If he interviewed GA, why not OA? If I were to go on his show, I reasoned, I could carry the message to a lot more people than we'd been able to reach so far by word of mouth.

At a meeting in mid-June, I told Jo, Barbara and the others who were there about my idea of going on the Paul Coates show. "Oh, it's too soon to go on television!" Jo and Barbara protested. "We don't have enough people yet. Just *our* weight loss isn't enough, Rozanne. We have to have a lot of people who've lost weight in OA for it to be an inspiration."

I argued strongly in favor of doing a show; surely our three stories would be an inspiration. Jo was equally strong in her opposition. "If you do it," she threatened, "I'm leaving!"

Nevertheless, I called the producer of the Paul Coates show and urged him to put me on television as a spokesperson for Overeaters Anonymous.

"Sorry," the producer told me. "We've already done two shows on obesity this year." One was about an early intestinal bypass operation; the other was a woman who'd lost 125 pounds with the help of a psychiatrist. "That's our quota for this year; call me back next year," he said.

Of course, I had no intention of waiting a year to call the producer again. I'd wait a month and see if his attitude had changed. I continued to promote the idea with Jo, Barbara and the others, and they continued to object.

Meanwhile, Jim was playing a key role for me as a friend and advisor. Because he had years of experience in AA and was GA's founder, I respected and valued his advice. He continued to urge me to call the producers.

During OA's first months we sometimes met at Jo's husband's office and sometimes in members' homes. Because there were so few of us—many weeks only three—we had no specific format. We would sit on sofas and chairs facing each other or in a semicircle, and just talk informally.

As time went by, I became dissatisfied with the way things were going. OA was turning into a weekly coffee klatch, and the basics of the program were hardly discussed. Personality conflicts were creeping in. After one disjointed, gossipy meeting, I was very upset and called Jim to ask for suggestions.

"How do you have the chairs arranged?" he asked when I described the problem. "Well, in a circle, more or less," I answered.

"Rozanne, I think it would work better if you'd set up the chairs theater style." "Theater style?" Now I was really confused.

He explained, "Put one chair for the leader at the front facing the group, and line up the other chairs in rows facing the leader. That kind of room arrangement discourages people from idle chatter and helps them focus on the program."

"But sometimes we only have three people," I protested.

"So, one of you be the leader and sit at the front, and the other two sit in a row facing the leader."

The next week I got to the meeting place early and set up the chairs theater style, with two little rows facing the leader. Appointing myself leader, I had a little table in front of my chair to put the guest book, where everybody signed in, and the literature.

By that time our literature consisted of one sheet with the rewritten Twelve Steps and the Serenity Prayer. Barbara had run off copies on the mimeograph machine at her office, and we proudly handed a sheet to anyone who came to our little group.

When the others arrived, they accepted the seating change gracefully. I had discussed Jim's advice with both Jo and Barbara during the week, and they had agreed that our meetings needed more structure. From that time on (as I would later write in *I Put My Hand In Yours*), the fundamentals of OA, because of their orderly presentation, became increasingly clearer and more meaningful to us.

Jim also came to talk to us several times during that first summer. Years later OA members who were in on those early meetings would remember Jim's warm, pleasant manner of speaking. He encouraged us to carry the message, to establish other OA groups and to live the program.

"Live it and you'll love it," he told us. "You won't know that you have lived until you have lived this way."

Barbara brought many friends to OA meetings that first year. Most of these only came for two or three meetings, but others became "regulars." I remember Netta H., the sister of Barbara's employer. Then there was Dorothy L., who had met Barbara at the health spa. Dorothy came off and on that first year, and in later years as well.

Twenty years later Dorothy recalled, "I remember Barbara driving me to my first meeting. That meeting was at someone's house, perhaps Jo's. There were two ladies who met us at the door and said something that made me welcome. There were chairs set up in the living room, folding chairs. At the front, to the right side, there was a card table with some typewritten pages on it."

Dorothy also remembered that Jo spoke first, welcoming the six or seven people in attendance to the meeting. "Then," she said, "you got up, Rozanne, and said that this group was just starting. It was inspired by GA and AA. But you also said . . . you felt each of you should go out, get a few people and start one [of your own]."

Dorothy, Barbara and Jo all remember those early OA meetings for the fellowship they experienced there, as well as the intimate sharing that went on during those two hours each Tuesday night. We talked a lot about our feelings, our families, and the problems which made us want to run to the refrigerator.

This atmosphere of emotional intimacy was OA's greatest strength. Unfortunately, sometimes it drove away those who were afraid of this kind of sharing. Dorothy remembers how, at one meeting, a woman got up and talked about her dying daughter. "We all cried," Dorothy said, "and I left and didn't come back. I couldn't take it."

For most of us, however, the freedom to share our feelings and problems was an essential factor in our recovery. Hand in hand, strengthened by mutual support, we were finding a way to cope with life without overeating.

By August Jo had gone from over 200 pounds to 109 pounds, dramatically altering her appearance. I clearly recall how she looked in late summer of 1960, gorgeous and slim in her form-fitting, red bathing suit. The weight loss had made a big change in her attitude toward life as well. Her marriage wasn't working out, and in August she and her husband divorced, and she left Los Angeles. She has never returned to OA.

Jo's departure left Barbara and me as OA's leaders and role models. Supposedly, we were the "authorities" on the program, the women to whom newcomers could look as proof that it worked.

Since we'd been meeting at Jo's husband's office and at each other's homes, we had no need for money. Therefore, we didn't pass a basket for donations. We had no formal group officers, not even a secretary or a treasurer. Our only format was reading our version of the Twelve Steps at the beginning of each meeting, and ending the meetings with the Serenity Prayer.

Women continued to come and go, and the group stayed small, with no more than five or ten at our Tuesday night meetings. Almost everyone resisted what Barbara and I had to offer. A few kept coming back. Although Jim spoke at our little meetings occasionally, we OAs were solely a Fellowship of women during our first two and a half years.

All through that long, hot summer and into the fall, I continued to pester the staff of the Paul Coates television show. Dan Fowler, one of the writers on the show, was particularly sympathetic to our cause. He thought the idea had merit, but the show's schedule didn't allow for us. By October I was beginning to despair. Would we ever hear from them again?

Then everything happened at once! It was ten o'clock one Friday night in late October, and we were all in bed. Suddenly the phone rang, and I stumbled through the darkened living room to answer it.

"Hello, Rozanne?" the voice on the other end asked. "This is Dan Fowler from the Paul Coates show. Can you be down here on Tuesday?"

It turned out that Paul Coates was leaving for Europe, and he had to tape three weeks' worth of shows ahead of time. There was room for us. Could we do it?

Instantly awake and barely hiding my excitement, I said, "Barbara and I will be there."

"Not just the two of you," replied Dan. "We want all seven of you, so we can pan across the others at the beginning of the show. Then Paul will interview you and Barbara." Despite my enthusiasm, I was dismayed. Only Barbara and I had lost weight. The others were still fat. What kind of impression would that make? I tried briefly to talk him out of it, but he was adamant. All of us or no one.

"Oh, yes," I hastily assured him. "We'll all be there. Thank you for asking us. Just tell me what time and where you want us."

After we hung up, I could scarcely contain myself. I called Barbara to tell her. She wasn't too happy about the publicity, and she definitely wasn't thrilled with the arrangements I'd been asked to make for the show. After much coaxing, she did agree that we needed more members and that this might be our only chance. Excited and hopeful, we hung up to call the others.

In 1960, Paul Coates was very famous, a nationally-syndicated journalist and television interviewer. To appear on his show would be a thrill for all of us.

By that time I'd been to enough AA meetings to know something about anonymity, although I still didn't fully understand the concept. I remembered the Gamblers Anonymous interview two years before, when the man had turned his back to the camera. Now I knew why: the Eleventh Tradition of never allowing a member's face to be shown in any public medium of communication. Still, I was uncertain. If we appeared on television full face, we would be breaking that important Tradition. Yet I felt we had to show our weight loss. It was a puzzle; what should we do?

I called Barbara that weekend. "Compulsive overeating is a visible illness," I told her, "and TV is a visual medium. If we're ever going to get OA off the ground, we have to go on full face. We don't have a choice." Then I added, "I'll do it this once, and I'll never do it again." Barbara agreed with me. We compromised by not allowing either our first or last names to be used, even during the interview. True to my word, I have never allowed my face to be shown on television since then.

The Coates call had come on Friday night, and on Monday I rented a post office box in a small neighborhood station. P.O. Box 3372, Beverly Hills, California was the address we would give out on the TV show. Writing the check to pay for the box was a major step for me. Hope and fear combined to set my heart pounding. Were we really on our way? (I didn't know it at the time, but that little box was to be OA's mailing address for the next twelve years.)

There were seven of us, the entire membership of Overeaters Anonymous, on that Tuesday night, November 1, 1960. We arrived at the studio in Hollywood and were ushered to the set of the show, where we were seated in a row of chairs facing the camera. The program opened with the camera focusing on each of the seven women, one by one, while Paul Coates dramatically spoke of us as victims of a "distorted and destructive compulsion—overeating," who had an unusual story to tell.

Following a commercial break, Coates introduced Barbara and me, without using our names, as hopeful actresses who had "watched their careers be destroyed because of an inability to stop from consuming great quantities of food."

Chapter One

Although Dan Fowler had been with us all along in this venture, it was Rollin Post, another writer on the Coates staff, who actually wrote that program. Before the telecast, Rollin talked to us at length about compulsive overeating, the OA program and what we were trying to accomplish. His questions grasped the situation completely and enabled Paul Coates to guide Barbara and me in getting our message across to television viewers. Coates began the interview by asking us to define the term "compulsive eater," to which I answered, "One who eats without any feeling of control, without caring about the consequences, who eats whether or not he or she is hungry or isn't hungry, who is seeking to destroy himself or herself in one way or another." Barbara added that a compulsive eater "will buy food without anyone knowing . . . will eat in secret, and will eat large quantities, abnormal quantities."

Coates asked us more about our eating patterns. He questioned our sneaking food, hiding food, lying about food. He asked about the weight loss methods we'd tried and about the emotional problems that might have caused us to become compulsive about food.

In answer to his questions, we discussed the disease of compulsive overeating. We talked about our need for comfort, our feelings of guilt and our powerlessness to stop. Barbara related her experience of sitting at the kitchen table bingeing and reading an article about weight reduction in a magazine, wishing she could look like the woman in the picture. "Yet I was eating," she said, "and I felt that there was no pleasure attached to it."

Then we talked a little bit about the OA Fellowship. I briefly discussed the founding of Overeaters Anonymous, referring to the founders in the third person in order to preserve the spirit of anonymity as much as possible. I said, "It started with two young women meeting by chance. One of us was informed of the activities of one of the other Anonymous organizations, and it was she who looked around, tried to find a group, and inevitably found one person who felt the way she did."

At one point Coates asked us how overeating could be treated with the same principles as those used by AA and GA. "You can keep a person away from gambling, and you can keep him away from whisky," he wondered, "but you can't keep him away from eating. This is an essential of life. [Do you] have to use a different kind of therapy [for your members] than Alcoholics Anonymous does?"

The word "abstinence" had yet to enter the OA vocabulary, but we had given much thought to this. "It's a slower process," I answered. "I feel that each compulsive eater knows where his or her own line of black and white is, the things that he or she can eat that will set him off on a binge and the things he can eat that won't set him off on a binge. I think in this manner it can be compared with alcoholism and gambling. A compulsive overeater knows how far he or she can go."

When Coates asked why our membership was limited to seven people, I spoke quite frankly of the many women who had come and gone during the nine months we'd been meeting. "Food is a crutch," I said, "and it's hard to give it up. This is the greatest battle I've ever fought, a *very* difficult thing to do, and some people are not up to it." He asked us if our members were married or single, how our husbands reacted to our membership, if we had any specific rules we followed.

We answered as carefully as we could, describing our Twelve-Step program of recovery and relating it to Alcoholics Anonymous.

He went on, "What do you do to encourage people who come into your organization?"

"We offer our own hope, our own courage and our own experiences," I replied. "This is the most we can do."

We discussed some of the spiritual principles upon which the OA program is based, the spirit of humility, the unconditional acceptance of others and finally of oneself. "When you can accept yourself," I added, "you often don't have to overeat."

We emphasized the many calls we made to each other

between meetings to help us stay away from the refrigerator. Answering his question, Barbara said she had lost fifty-six pounds, and I told him I'd lost forty-five pounds.

"Is Overeaters Anonymous equipped to expand?" Coates asked us. We assured him we were. "We welcome anyone with the same problem," I added, "anyone with a desire to stop overeating."

"Any money involved?" he queried. We told him we were self-supporting, with no dues or fees.

"Do you have any thoughts of permitting men into the organization?" he wanted to know.

"As the group grows, I think there will be men," Barbara answered. "Or if they are uncomfortable, there can be off-shoot organizations of men only."

Finally he asked me, "Well now, if there are people who are interested in learning more about this . . . how do they get in touch with you?"

I felt my heart beating faster. "They can write to Overeaters Anonymous, Post Office Box 3372, Beverly Hills, California."

Then Paul Coates added in closing, "And if they're from outside of the state of California, you can advise them on how to start their own group. . . ."

This was our first hint that Paul Coates' Confidential File might be more than just a local program. Our second hint came from Rollin Post, who greeted us warmly as we were leaving. "Thank you, ladies," he smiled. "You did a wonderful job. We'll let you know when it plays in the other cities."

"Other cities?" I repeated incredulously. "You mean this isn't just a Los Angeles show?"

"No, it's shown on stations in Sacramento, San Francisco, Tucson, Minneapolis and Tampa."

We were speechless! We had no meetings in those other places. What if somebody wrote to us from Tucson or Tampa needing help? We had no idea what to do. "Oh, well," Barbara and I told each other, "we'll think of something. We already told them we had nothing to offer but our own experience. We do have experience in starting an OA group, so we can tell them how to do that."

Rollin Post said the show would air in Los Angeles on Thanksgiving Eve, and we assumed that would be its first showing.

In the meantime, I treasured our new little post office box. Every day I went into Beverly Hills just to look at that empty box. One day, a week before the show was due to run in Los Angeles, I saw an envelope in the box folded around something else. I thought, "That's interesting. Someone from the post office must have seen our registration slip and written us a little letter." So I opened the box and pulled out the envelope. Suddenly, the floor was flooded! I just stood there, flabbergasted, looking at the sea of mail.

That envelope had been folded around fifty other letters. Thanksgiving was still a week away; where had all this mail come from? As I sorted through the letters at home, it was clear that the telecast had run in San Francisco and Sacramento, but we hadn't been notified. Those fifty letters were only the beginning.

After the interview showed on Thanksgiving Eve in Los Angeles, the response increased and our excitement mounted. Every day I went back to the post office in Beverly Hills with my little girls to check the box.

The mail continued to pour in over the next two months as the program aired in Minneapolis, Tucson and Tampa. From that one Paul Coates interview, we eventually received more than five hundred letters.

At last, Overeaters Anonymous was on its way!

Chapter Two

You Are
Not Alone

ETWEEN our taping of the Paul Coates show and the Los Angeles telecast on Thanksgiving Eve, I had an important conversation with Jim W., our long-suffering friend and Gamblers Anonymous founder.

"Oh, Jim," I enthused over the phone, "last night we were interviewed by Paul Coates. Isn't that terrific?" There was a small silence. "Jim, did you hear me?"

"I heard you, Rozanne, and I think it's wonderful." Another silence. Then he dropped his bombshell. "Rozanne," he went on, "let's talk about your Twelve Steps. You know, I think you ought to put back the spiritual. Separate the physiological from the spiritual. Put the physiological where it belongs in the introduction to the discussion of your program, and put God back into the Twelve Steps the way AA has them."

I dug in my heels and stubbornly refused. He took a deep breath and began again. "Listen, Rozanne," he coaxed, "if you *could* have done it by yourself, you *would* have done it by yourself. But all your life you've depended on doctors, fad diets and pills. These are all powers outside of you. Now," he went on, "you have a meeting every week and you talk to someone every day. Don't you see that these are powers outside of you, too?" Hesitantly, I agreed.

His next few statements were to change my life forever. "Rozanne," he persisted, "why don't you take the capital 'P' off of Power and make it a small 'p.' Then say to yourself, 'I'm *willpowerless* over food.' Can you do that?"

With that phrase Jim had captured my attention. "Willpower" was a dieter's term. All my life I'd said, "I have no willpower." Now I could admit to being willpowerless over food without having to admit to a belief in a Higher Power. Without my realizing it, Jim had opened the door to a spiritual belief for me. I still couldn't step over that threshold, but the time was coming.

At that moment, however, I wasn't quite ready for a full change to AA's exact wording of the Steps. I decided to wait while I gave the matter some thought.

Meanwhile, the letters from our appearance on Paul Coates' Confidential File were pouring into our little post office box. Juanita K. (one of our seven OA members), Barbara and I met to discuss the situation. What should we do first? How should we handle the mail?

Juanita and Barbara were working full time. In addition, Barbara had a husband and a teenage daughter to care for. The intensity level in my house was unbelievable. My husband had to be at work at eight o'clock in the morning, and he came home at six o'clock for dinner. My little Debbie was barely three-and-a-half and had just started nursery school. Julie was only twenty months old and was still in diapers. Confusion reigned supreme. I wasn't even writing to my mother in Chicago when I was supposed to; how could I possibly answer all these letters?

It wouldn't be enough just to reply to the letters. We would need a permanent method of keeping track of all OA correspondence. In addition, we would need a central place from which to conduct our business.

Because Barbara and the others were working in offices, and I had to be at home for my two babies, my little ten-by-ten-foot dining room became the embryonic beginning of today's World Service Office. I called it our General Service Office (GSO) because that's what AA called its headquarters in New York.

Earlier that year I had bought a sturdy typewriter table and a new Royal Magic Margin typewriter. I set them up in a corner of my dining room. (My trusty manual typewriter was to serve me well for the next four busy years, until it finally died in the service of OA and was replaced by a new electric machine.) Now that I had the tools I needed, I was ready for action. My secretarial training and office experience proved invaluable as we began to set up an efficient system for answering the mail.

Of the seven women who had appeared on the Coates show November first, five remained after Thanksgiving. After the first three shows ran, Netta H., Juanita, Beverly, Barbara and I called everyone in the greater Los Angeles area who had sent us a telephone number. Their reaction was enthusiastic, and we invited them all to our next Tuesday night meeting.

In anticipation of the new people, I had scurried around trying to find a meeting room. We had no idea how many would come, and of course the initial financial outlay would have to be borne by the five of us.

I settled on the Beverly Hills YMCA. We rented their main auditorium for fifteen dollars, a large sum in those days.

Juanita, Barbara and I were trying to stay calm, but we alternated periods of pragmatic efficiency with overwhelming excitement. Would people be interested? Would they respond? Most important, would they want to join in making Overeaters Anonymous a strong and effective organization for compulsive overeaters?

On Tuesday, November 29, 1960, we held our first meeting after the Coates telecasts. It was incredible! All year we'd struggled along with two to ten members. The prior Tuesday we'd had five members; that night seventy-five people came to hear what we had to offer.

As usual, we put a table at the front of the room where people could sign in and pick up copies of our original, rewritten Twelve Steps and the Serenity Prayer. We still had no Traditions (more about that later). At eight o'clock Barbara and I walked up on the stage at the front of the auditorium, where we had set up a small table and two chairs. We looked at each other, then out at the audience. "Here we go," I whispered to her as the two of us opened the meeting. It was a memorable night for both of us—facing all those strangers, offering faith, hope and the experience we'd had with the OA program.

"My name is Rozanne, and I'm a compulsive overeater," I began. "Last January I weighed 161 pounds, and tonight I weigh 113 pounds. I want to share with you this wonderful thing that has happened to me," I said. I talked about my own eating history and how OA had come into being just ten months before. Barbara told some of her story, too. Then we shared our vision for OA, how it could grow and help compulsive overeaters all over the world. We encouraged people who lived a distance from West Los Angeles to start new OA groups.

The audience was very quiet, listening attentively. As was our custom, the meeting lasted two hours with a break about halfway through.

Just before the break we passed a basket. We explained about the tremendous expenses and how the five of us had financed everything up to that point. We also talked about the financial outlay to come as we answered all of the letters. People were very generous that night. In addition, many others sent dimes and quarters when requesting information. The first thirty OA members eventually financed carrying the message to the five hundred who had written to us after the TV shows.

During the meeting break, Barbara and I were overwhelmed with questioning people. It was obvious that we had met a real need. The enthusiasm was contagious, and we were both very encouraged.

In the audience that night were several women who would soon become active in OA and have a vital impact on the development of our Fellowship. One of these was Lorraine Z., a delightful lady who always had a smile for everyone. When the meeting was over, she came up to me at the table and said, "Hi, Rozanne. I'm Lorraine, and I'm going to join your group. My husband and I have our own printing business. Could you use some help? If you need any printing done, we'll be glad to do it for you at a nominal cost."

I was overjoyed and quickly accepted her offer. Barbara had been mimeographing my writing at her office, but I wanted our pamphlets to have a more polished appearance. Up to that time we hadn't thought about what to do next; we'd just been making do with what we had.

Now, here was our first miracle. We desperately needed an economical and expert printing service. I wanted to write a pamphlet explaining OA as we would if we could personally visit with each of the suffering compulsive overeaters who had written to us. We also wanted to give information about the Fellowship, the Steps, and about how to set up and conduct OA meetings. Suddenly, effortlessly, our printing problem had been solved!

After people had left, Barbara and I looked at each other. Elated and hopeful, we said to one another, "What do you think? Did we succeed?" But the response had left no doubt: OA's growth had begun that very night. Calming down the next day, we knew the real work was about to begin.

The following evening I sat down at my typewriter to compose our very first piece of OA literature. It was a four-page, 8½-by-11-inch booklet containing an introductory page about OA, a second page with the newly-revised Twelve Steps, a third page with a little history of OA, and a fourth page introducing our Twelve Unifying Rules (the forerunner of today's Twelve Traditions). This booklet was the beginning of my many attempts over the years to extend a helping hand to other compulsive overeaters through the written word.

Even today, some OA groups in various parts of the world are using a portion of that original pamphlet in their meeting formats, not knowing its origins.

True to her offer, Lorraine's company, Mitchell Letter Mart, Inc., printed this brochure and continued to support and guide our printing efforts for the next seven years.

Following is the front page of the booklet, written in December, 1960, which those first five hundred people received:

OVEREATERS ANONYMOUS— HOW IT CAN HELP YOU

Overeaters Anonymous is a fellowship of men and women who meet to share their experience, strength and hope with each other that they may solve their common problem and help others to recover from the self-destruction of compulsive overeating.

The only requirement for membership is an honest desire to stop overeating and to effect a change in eating habits. Before embarking on this program, our experience has taught us to seek the aid of a physician of our own choosing, returning to him for regular checkups. We have found that he, and only he, can advise us regarding our own calorie allotments and wisest nutritional program.

Most of us have been unwilling to admit that we were real problem overeaters. No one likes to think he is different from his fellows. Therefore, our lives have been spent in countless vain attempts to lose weight and to prove we could eat like other people. Some of us, on rare occasions, even attained our normal weight. However, sooner or later we always found ourselves on the way to an even greater increase in weight than before. The old compulsion always returned, bringing with it the same unhappy feelings of guilt, rejection, loneliness and despair that had always accompanied our periods of overeating. In reality we had lost the ability to control our eating without outside help.

We know now that no true compulsive overeater ever maintains permanent control on his own. We are convinced that overeaters of our nature are in the grip of a progressive illness. Left to our own devices we seem only to become worse, never better.

Within the fellowship of Overeaters Anonymous we find that we are not alone. Here we can bring our feelings out into the open. Here we find willing ears and sympathetic hearts;

people who are not judging us for our actions but who have suffered as we have and are ready to share their strength as we make the long journey back to recovery. We discover that we help ourselves most by helping others with the same problem. We learn that we must honestly admit to our innermost selves that we are compulsive overeaters. This is the first step toward recovery.

The prime concern of OA is not with diets, calories and weight, but with the feelings that lie behind our overeating, even the everyday occasions that tend to make us seek excess food. We have learned that regular meetings are essential in encouraging self-discipline, that mid-meeting telephone calls have sustained more than one faltering member on the verge of returning to unhappy habits. We have recognized the vital importance of taking only one day at a time, only one pound at a time. Often just the postponement of the desired food for only one minute will lead to more determined postponement for one hour, one day, and miraculously . . . postponement forever.

Since we have admitted that we are "power-less" to control our eating, we have learned to place our faith and trust in a Power greater than ourselves. For some this Power may be a religious God, for others it may merely mean the power and strength of OA as a whole. Whatever our beliefs, we are constantly striving for humility, self-understanding and self-acceptance—the most vital elements in our struggle for self-control.

As a positive program toward controlling our compulsive overeating we faithfully read, think about and practice to the best of our ability the following twelve steps, which we consider the basis of our program of recovery.

Unaware of copyright restrictions, I borrowed parts of this writing from the AA "Big Book." However, most of our first page came from my heart in my own words.

Satisfied with my explanation of how OA could help the compulsive overeater, I turned my attention to rewriting my Twelve Steps (again!).

The second page was to contain those revised Twelve Steps. I had been thinking seriously about what Jim had said earlier that month. Each time I talked to him, he would urge me to reconsider my position on the Steps. Slowly, I began to agree that he was probably right, and that if I wanted OA to be like AA and GA, I would have to make OA's Twelve Steps more like theirs.

Remembering his admonition to separate the physiological from the spiritual, and to put all physical information in the introduction to the description of our program, I gave in and took his advice. I removed my original Step Two about seeking the aid of a physician and placed it on the first page of the new brochure.

On the second page of our new booklet, I presented the Twelve Steps of Overeaters Anonymous. They were the introduction to our recovery program for the first five hundred men and women who came into OA following the Paul Coates interview:

THE TWELVE STEPS

1. We admit that we are compulsive overeaters . . . that our lives have become unmanageable.
2. We admit that we need help—that a Power greater than ourselves can restore us to a normal way of thinking and living.
3. We have gradually learned to place our complete faith and trust in this Power.
4. We shall make a searching and fearless moral inventory of ourselves.
5. We will admit to ourselves and to another human being the exact nature of our difficulties.
6. We are entirely ready to have these defects of character removed.
7. We humbly ask God (of our understanding) to help us remove our shortcomings.
8. We shall make a list of all persons we have hurt through our actions and gradually become willing to make amends to them.
9. As we grow stronger within ourselves we shall willingly make amends to these people by changing our attitudes and actions toward them.

10. We will continue to take personal inventory, and when we are wrong, promptly admit it.
11. We shall seek through prayer and meditation to improve our conscious contact with God as we understand Him, praying only for knowledge of His will for us and the strength to carry that out.
12. Having gained a spiritual awareness as a result of these steps, we shall try to practice them in all our affairs and to carry this message to other compulsive overeaters.

Notice that these Steps were still being written in the present and future tenses, since we had barely any past. This also reflected that none of us had yet worked through the Steps. They were still not exactly like AA's Steps. GA's phrase about "normal way of thinking and living" remained, although I had moved it from my original Step Three into Step Two.

Surrender and spiritual awakening were still beyond me, so I found more acceptable ways (in my opinion) to phrase Steps Three and Twelve. I also didn't see the necessity of making direct amends, so Step Nine avoids the issue.

In essence, these Steps showed that God was our helper and that we were in control. It was to be another twenty months before we really followed AA's path.

By the end of 1960, we could look back on nearly a year of weight loss, recovery, experience and hope. It was important that all those calling and writing know what had happened to us and what we hoped to achieve in the future.

Therefore, my next task was to write the third page of our booklet describing our Fellowship:

OVEREATERS ANONYMOUS—
HOW IT CAME INTO BEING

The fellowship of Overeaters Anonymous is the outgrowth of a chance meeting between two young women in Los Angeles during the first week in January, 1960.

These women had a truly unhappy history of overeating . . . a compulsion which brought with it feelings of despair, loneliness and desperation. They began to meet regularly each week and to call one another by telephone nearly every day . . . each bringing to the other a measure of understanding, encouragement, faith and hope.

As the months passed, other people came to these meetings. Some, not yet ready for this step, did not return. However, at the end of ten months there were seven women, meeting regularly, who were facing their problem with ever-increasing hope and confidence.

These women concluded from their discussions that in order to prevent a return to the old habits it was necessary to bring about some personality changes within themselves. In order to accomplish this they used for a guide certain spiritual principles which had helped thousands of people who had recovered from other compulsive addictions. Most important, in order to maintain their own change in patterns of eating they felt that it was vitally necessary to carry the message of hope to other compulsive overeaters.

Finally, a prominent columnist and television commentator offered to interview these women in order to make their problem and its solution known to others. The response was overwhelming. The idea spread rapidly as many men and women sought an answer to this age-old compulsion.

Soon OA groups were flourishing in many other areas, for as long as there are people suffering from this unhappy affliction, there will be people who have overcome it and will share their strength and hope through the Fellowship of Overeaters Anonymous.

This page was the first OA history ever written, and the last paragraph represented my dream for myself and others like me.

The fourth page of our little booklet contained information brand new to Overeaters Anonymous. During our first year, after I originally rewrote the Twelve Steps and took out God as much as I could, we paid no attention to AA's Twelve Trad-itions. They were confusing to me and meant absolutely nothing. Besides, until taking my husband's friend to a meeting of Gambler's Anonymous, I had never had any contact with a Twelve-Step group at all.

By the end of that first year I had already been to two more GA meetings and many AA meetings. At all these places

I heard not only the Twelve Steps but the Twelve Traditions as well. I knew I had to address the issue of the Traditions for OA. But how?

I simply couldn't grasp the significance of that word, "Tradition." What did that mean? What did that have to do with us? I understood that these were unifying principles for AA. GA called them "The Unity Program," and since I didn't yet realize that AA had no rules, I decided to call them "The Twelve Unifying Rules."

Believing that I could improve the writing and clarity, I proceeded to rewrite AA's Traditions just as I had rewritten their Steps. On the fourth and last page of our new booklet, those first OA members learned how we planned to grow together.

THE TWELVE UNIFYING RULES

In order to maintain group unity, our experience has shown that:

1. Our common welfare should come first; personal recovery depends upon OA unity.
2. Our leaders do not rule us; they are but trusted members who merely serve.
3. The only requirement for OA membership is an honest desire to stop overeating and to effect a change in eating habits.
4. Each OA group has but one primary purpose—to carry its message to the overeater who still suffers.
5. There are no dues or fees for OA membership. Each group ought to be fully self-supporting through its members' contributions, declining outside donations.
6. Each group should be self-governing, except in matters affecting other groups or OA as a whole.
7. An OA group ought never endorse, finance or lend the OA name to any related facility or outside enterprise, lest problems of money, property and prestige divert us from our primary purpose of helping others.
8. OA is not allied with any sect, denomination, organization, institution or political party, does not wish to engage in any controversy, neither endorses nor opposes any causes. Hence the OA name ought never be drawn into public controversy.

9. OA should remain forever non-professional, the only workers being members themselves.
10. Overeaters Anonymous, as such, ought never be organized, but we may create service boards or committees directly responsible to those they serve.
11. Our public relations policy is based on attraction rather than promotion; we must always maintain personal anonymity at the level of press, radio, films, television and other media of communication.
12. Anonymity is the spiritual foundation of the OA program, ever reminding us to place humility before personal prestige.

I was still struggling with the concept of God, so I took out the first half of AA's Tradition Two about one ultimate authority. Our Second Unifying Rule said simply, "Our leaders do not rule us; they are but trusted members who merely serve."

Our Third Rule reflected the very reason I had started OA: "The only requirement for OA membership is an honest desire to stop overeating and to effect a change in eating habits."

Because the office was still in my little dining room and we only had volunteers to do the work, I didn't understand AA's phrase, "special workers." That's why our Ninth Unifying Rule talked about "the only workers being members themselves." I couldn't foresee a day when we would have our own office building with a full-time staff of both non-members and members.

Our Eleventh Rule reflected the rapid technological changes being made in communications. The Telstar satellite had just been sent up, and I knew the future held more developments in store. Therefore, when I read AA's "press, radio and films," I knew we needed to include more specifics. Thus I added ". . . television and other media of communication." That last phrase turned out to be a fortunate choice, as ever-increasing numbers of public-media options became available each year.

Finally, AA's "principles before personalities" made no

sense to me. "What are they talking about?" I asked myself. "I can say it more clearly." That's why our Twelfth Unifying Rule stated ". . . ever reminding us to place humility before personal prestige."

Reviewing the four pages I had written, I felt they said everything we wanted to convey to those who were asking about us. Later that week I showed the booklet to Barbara for her approval. After carefully reading it, she responded enthusiastically. "That's great, Rozanne," she said. "What about that lady who has the printing business? Do you think she can help us?"

"Oh, sure," I answered. "I'll call her right away." Never one to wait, I mailed a copy to Lorraine the next morning. True to her word, Lorraine made suggestions for layout and typeface, and we had several hundred brochures ready to mail within the week.

In the meantime, I knew I had to write an accompanying letter which would describe our situation and yet encourage people to join us. It was no small task. I had to find a way to help people to connect with each other, hopefully to start new OA groups in other areas. I'd need their permission to give out their names and addresses, and this all had to be accomplished with the initial letter. How could I achieve this goal?

After much thought, I had an inspiration! I'd include a form at the bottom of the letter where people could indicate whether they wanted to start a group or join one. We also invited Los Angeles-area people to call us for information. Forms similar to this are still effective in areas of the world where people are struggling to establish Overeaters Anonymous.

Here's the first letter we sent to those five hundred compulsive overeaters who wrote to us begging for help:

January, 1961
AN OPEN LETTER

To all of you who have written to us expressing your interest in Overeaters Anonymous . . . our heartfelt thanks and gratitude.

We offer our sincerest apologies for the delay in answering your letters, but the following explanation will help you to understand the situation:

When we appeared on the Paul Coates Show we were only seven women, all homemakers with children, working together to solve the problem we had been unable to cope with alone. We were completely unprepared for the response. To date we have been deluged with more than 400 letters from all over the country, each a despairing cry for help.

The enormity of our undertaking became increasingly apparent as the letters continued to pour in. From a very small group we grew overnight to a nationwide Fellowship of compulsive overeaters. Immediately, problems of drafting and printing information, setting up groups, and contacting people began to overwhelm us. Because there were only seven of us, everything took much longer than we anticipated, . . . yet slowly but surely OA began to grow in an orderly and constructive manner.

However, the problem of expenses plagued us all along. We were unprepared for the total cost of even such trivial items as postage—not to mention stationery supplies, post office box rentals, and most important, printing of the information you requested.

Our small Los Angeles group has been defraying all expenses up to now. As you will see from our Twelve Unifying Rules, we are self-supporting through our own contributions. However, contributions from the few here cannot begin to cover the cost of the many.

We are giving all of you this initial information without cost because we sincerely believe in helping one another. However, in the future we know you will understand that when you request additional copies of our program, there will be a nominal charge of 10 cents per copy to cover only the printing and mailing costs.

Enclosed with this letter is the information you requested. In reading it thoroughly, you will find the answers to everything you have asked us about the OA program.

Most of you are unaware that within your area are many fellow sufferers who are eagerly looking for someone with whom to start this program. In order to bring you together, we ask your cooperation in the following manner:

Please indicate in the proper boxes below whether you are interested in starting a group in your area or whether you prefer to join a group being started by someone else. If you wish to start an OA group, we shall then send you a list of the people nearest you who have written to us. If you wish to join a group we shall send you the name of your nearest volunteer group-starter.

In the beginning this may take quite a bit of your time. Please don't let that discourage you nor shake your faith and determination. The information you send us on these forms is urgently needed in order to bring you all together in the most effective manner. We hope you will return them to us as soon as possible.

As we begin our second year of existence, we can assure you that OA is a workable program which is proving itself more and more successful every day. It is no quick miracle but a gradual, steady proof of the fact that compulsive overeaters can share their problems and help each other to the benefit of themselves, their families and the communities in which they live.

In all humility, we hope you will help us by letting us help you.

☐ I wish to start an OA group in my area. Please send me the names, addresses and phone numbers of people near me. I will contact them and keep you informed of our progress as an OA group.

☐ I wish to join an OA group. Please send me the name, address and phone number of the group-starter nearest me.

NAME: _____

ADDRESS: _____

PHONE NO: _____

Please be sure to enclose a self-addressed, stamped, legal-size envelope (the same size as the envelope in which you received this letter).

NOTE TO PEOPLE IN THE LOS ANGELES AREA: If you will give us your telephone number, we will be happy to call you to inform you of the day, time and place of our weekly meetings.

Carrying the Message

THE week after our first open meeting was exciting and hectic for all of us from the original little group.

Barbara still had to go to her office every day. I had Marvin and my two little girls to care for, and the other five women also had family and job responsibilities.

Fortunately, the filing system Juanita, Barbara and I had set up was proving its worth. As the letters came in, a card was made up for each inquiry so that we would have an accurate record. Those cards are part of OA's archives today.

After the first meeting, our telephones rang constantly. The chaos in our homes was unbelieveable. Eventually, Barbara had to put a second phone in her home. As soon as she came home from work, Barbara told me, she would fix dinner with one hand and hold the phone with the other. I could (barely!) juggle laundry, ironing, meals, children and phone calls all at the same time. According to Barbara, "I answered all the telephone calls, day and night until three o'clock in the morning, and I then had to go to work the next morning."

How did our families accept this? Barbara's husband and daughter were very unhappy about the many hours she spent talking to so many strangers. "Are you the only one who can help?" they'd complain. "Where are the others?"

Well, I was the only "other." If Marvin suffered, he did it

silently. My dear husband has been supportive since the very beginning. Never once did he issue an ultimatum as husbands of other OA members would later do: "It's me or OA; make your choice!" I would hold phone conversations and care for my family during the day and evening. Then every night from seven-thirty until midnight, I'd write OA literature and answer letters. Young and energetic, I was obsessed with my new idea and determined to have OA succeed.

As time went on, OA became woven into the fabric of my life, and Barbara confessed to having the same feelings. So much happened so fast that sometimes we couldn't tell where marriage and motherhood ended and OA began.

Meanwhile, our lone OA group continued every Tuesday night. Prior to November 29, we'd been unsure of the response we would have to the Coates telecasts. Therefore, we had only arranged for one meeting at the Beverly Hills YMCA. Just imagine our stunned reaction to the jam-packed room that night!

During the coffee break I whispered to Barbara, "Where will we meet next week?" "Don't worry," she reassured me, "we can meet at my house for awhile. My living room is really big." At that first meeting we'd had seventy-five people. The second meeting in Barbara's living room drew twenty-five people, and from these we developed a core group of members who began attending regularly and working the OA program as we had written it then.

It was an interesting time of year for everyone to begin this new venture. Chanukah, Christmas and New Year's Eve lay just ahead. Could we all meet this challenge during such a traditional overeating-binge period? While some succumbed to temptation, others managed to survive the holidays without overeating. We saw that the Steps really did work, that the meetings and phone calls were supportive. We passed our first major holiday test with flying colors!

By early January our four-page brochure and Open Letter were printed. Sending them out required a mass mailing. For this task we took over Barbara's living room, where we pushed her furniture against the walls and set up several long tables down the entire length of the room.

Using the little index cards I'd made up as the letters arrived, we assembled the materials to be mailed, filled in the mailing date on each card and addressed envelopes to the hundreds of suffering compulsive overeaters who had written.

Barbara had always been more successful than I was at bringing in new OA members from among her friends and coworkers. Now she tried to recruit as many as she could to come help stuff envelopes. Despite her efforts, there were only four or five of us, including Juanita, Netta, Barbara and me, to do the bulk of the work in answering all that mail. A smattering of new members also came to help after the holidays had passed.

Printing, office supplies, postage, post office box rental and all other expenses for all this correspondence came from the money collected in the meeting basket (after we'd paid the fifteen dollars weekly rental to the Temple) and from our own pockets.

What an exciting and hectic period that was for all of us! The original little group of seven had expanded to twenty-five or thirty. We were all feeling our way, trying to help one another, and at the same time banding together to answer all those heartbreaking appeals for help. We could sense that OA was poised on the verge of rapid growth. In fact, as OA entered its second year of existence, we were too busy spreading the message to even remember our first birthday on January 19, 1961.

Near the end of January our intense efforts reached a triumphant conclusion; we had answered all the letters—nearly five hundred!

On January 20, 1961, I wrote to Sybil W., (Jim W.'s wife) who was secretary of the Los Angeles AA office:

Dear Sybil:
Enclosed you will find all the information which we

mailed today to over 450 people who have written to us in the last two months.

Since you and your co-workers have been kind enough to refer people to us who have called at your Central Service Office, we felt you ought to have a copy of our program for your files.

As of this date (before the mailing), we have a membership of approximately 35 women. At least 20 of them have really caught the spirit of the group in the last seven weeks since our first meeting, and I would say we have about 25 or so who have been returning steadily. It's really most encouraging and gratifying, as you well know.

We all wish to extend our thanks to you, to Jim, and to all of those in AA and GA who have blazed the trail for us to follow and explore.

God bless you all.

After all the letters were mailed, we didn't have to wait long for answers from compulsive overeaters. Phone calls came in immediately; written replies started showing up within a few days. A few people wanted to start groups in their areas; most wanted to join an existing group.

During this second round of responses, we handled each one individually. It was very time-consuming, but necessary. In many personal letters, most of which I wrote myself, we shared information about other people we'd heard from who lived near the letter-writer, as well as people who were starting groups. Of course, no names, addresses or phone numbers were given out unless we had prior permission. The promise of privacy was very important to me, even at that early date.

Suddenly, just as I'd hoped it would, the OA Fellowship began to spread! Three young women from the San Fernando Valley, just over the hill from Los Angeles, had attended that first meeting after the Paul Coates show. They had immediately caught the enthusiasm Barbara and I had for OA. Week after week, they drove in for our Tuesday night meetings. Those were the days before freeways were everywhere, so the only ways over the hill were a few long, winding canyon roads which connected the Valley and Los Angeles. That was our first evidence that members would be willing to go to any lengths for recovery.

Mary L. was a pretty young girl with a serious weight problem. She believed OA held the answer for her. "But it's just too far to drive, Rozanne," she told me one day. "I'm going to start a group in Panorama City." Courageously she followed through, and her group became OA Group Number Two, the first of hundreds in the San Fernando Valley.

Meanwhile, we'd had considerable correspondence with Jean R. in Fairfax, Marin County. This was a beautiful area north of San Francisco in Northern California. Jean had written to us on November 16, right after seeing the Paul Coates interview. In that first letter, she said:

> It seemed like providence, because our T.O.P.S. chapter, last night, decided to resign from the 'national' group and organize a local group-therapy club. When you mentioned the 12 Steps . . . I realized your organization was following the AA pattern, with which I have had some experience. Our 20 or more members are convinced that a fellowship or group therapy plan can help us lose weight and re-educate our eating habits. If you can offer us any guidance of method, we would be most grateful.

On January 20, 1961, I sent Jean our new brochure and Open Letter. I also wrote her a separate letter and invited her group to become the "Fairfax branch of Overeaters Anonymous." She answered that on February 1 her group had met with a man who had written to us and who wanted to organize OA in Marin County. They decided to join OA as our Group Number Three, the first in Northern California. We referred to her the names of other people who had written to us from Marin County, and soon that group was flourishing.

Jean and others in faraway locations were in desperate need of guidance in organizing and conducting OA meetings. As soon as we answered the first round of letters, I began work on a meeting format to be printed and distributed to those starting new OA groups. This was information we would have given them if we could have been there to help them in person, knowledge we'd gathered during our year of trial and error in the original group.

This format had not been printed yet when Jean wrote me again, frantic for more help. Taking time out to write her another long letter on February 20, I explained our delay in getting materials distributed and gave her a short version of the format to come. This letter is the earliest description of how we were conducting our Tuesday night meetings at that time:

1. Set up the chairs auditorium-style with the meeting leader seated at a table in front of the group. We have found that just sitting in a circle tends to promote idle chit-chat and personality conflicts.

2. At the beginning of each meeting we read completely each part of the OA program: How OA Can Help You, the 12 Steps, the OA History, the 12 Unifying Rules, and the Serenity Prayer. The leader chooses a different person for each part, and this person comes to the front of the group and reads aloud. It seems to help all of us to hear these things every week; I guess we all need the reinforcement and reminder of what we are and how we can help ourselves.

3. Each member then speaks about herself and her problem. We do not discuss diets or calories, but rather our feelings about food and our attitudes, past and present, toward everything that relates to our common compulsion.

4. These speeches are limited to five minutes. This gives everyone a chance to talk and prevents the meeting from going off on a tangent. We time them, and the person timing for that night rings a little bell at the end of the five minutes. The speaker then finishes as quickly as possible.

5. During the speeches we ask that there be absolutely no interruptions, comments or undercurrents of talk. If necessary, we repeat this during the evening. It is important that every member be given a chance to speak her heart, to tell of what is troubling her without any interruption at all.

6. After everyone has spoken, we all rise to repeat the Serenity Prayer in unison.

7. When the formal meeting is concluded, we hold our General Discussion. The leader still leads this, making sure there is no babble or discourtesy during the questions and answers. This is the period in which we encourage anyone to ask questions of any kind. They could relate to questions about OA, overeating, more specific questions about how to serve non-tempting foods at a party a member might be giving, how to handle oneself at restaurants or social affairs, how to cope with anger or frustration without eating, suggestions about doing marketing right after mealtime instead of just before, etc. It is also the time when members stand to ask for phone numbers in their area, or to mention that they might need a ride to the meetings. We encourage people to stand and ask their questions, though it isn't necessary. However, even at this time we don't discuss diets or calories or weights. We do, however, encourage more specific questions about the conquering of overeating, since the spiritual side is usually covered in the individual speeches.

8. When there are no more questions to be asked, we then close the meeting, and everyone is free to mingle and make friends.

9. I had forgotten to mention that immediately after the close of the formal meeting, we have a treasurer's report and pass the basket. No one is required to contribute, or to "make up" for unattended meetings. Since our group is large enough to necessitate renting a room for the meetings, we must collect enough to pay for this rental. Since each OA group is self-governing, if you have no expenses, then there would be no reason for contributions. At this point we have enough money (just barely!) to cover printing costs for the near future, so there would be no reason to contribute anything more to us. We do thank you very much for your check for $5. It was most gratefully received, I assure you.

In addition to the long hours I was spending on correspondence, both Barbara and I continued to put in even more hours on the telephone. Because we had been the leaders during the first year and had been interviewed by Paul Coates, many OA newcomers regarded the two of us as stars and experts. There were no OA sponsors in those days, so we found ourselves more or less sponsoring everyone in our rapidly-growing Fellowship.

As Barbara would later remember: "Everyone seemed to want help; they wanted people to talk to them for hours. The phones were going constantly. It was difficult because we didn't have other successful people, and so the only people they were calling were Rozanne and me. We were inundated with calls for a long time. We encouraged people to call each other, but they only wanted to call people who were successful. That was a difficult period. I took in an extra phone. Until one or two o'clock at night I had two- and three-hour conversations with people. The return was wonderful, but I felt really frightened to be getting all these calls. People were looking for help, and I felt like anything I said or did became godlike to them."

Barbara and I also continued to lead the meeting every Tuesday night through the early months of 1961. When we tried to step aside and get others to lead meetings, we got complaints. According to Barbara, "There were some people that were not warm people. They did not hold an audience. Then we got a lot of dissatisfaction. People called and said, 'I didn't like the meeting.' They weren't getting the same enthusiasm out of it. We had to jump in [and take the lead again]."

On April 8 we were finally able to mail out a formal, printed meeting format to people interested in starting OA meetings. That original format was titled "Overeaters Anonymous: General Information and Procedure for Weekly Meetings." In seven pages it repeats and elaborates upon the information which was given briefly to Jean R. by letter about how to set up chairs and organize meetings. Much other material was added as well. We included information about speaking procedures at meetings, meeting leaders, the importance of quiet during the entire meeting and between-meeting telephone calls. Under the heading of "Membership

Requirements" was the statement, "Overeaters Anonymous is open to anyone who is a compulsive overeater. Weight is never a criterion."

One theme which runs through the writings is the concept of discipline. From our disorganized early OA meetings, we had worked out, step by step, methodical conduct for the Tuesday night group. This gave us all a sense of security and insured that everybody would get the most possible information, inspiration and support from those two hours we spent together each week. Also, it seemed to us that order in meetings and order in eating habits went together. People who came to OA with out-of-control eating and living habits often began to gain a sense of self-control and self-respect as they disciplined themselves to stand up in the front of the room when speaking at our OA meetings or to keep quiet when others were speaking.

The suggested meeting format mailed to all group-starters included seven announcements which we read aloud at the beginning of every Tuesday night OA meeting. Most of these dealt with various aspects of anonymity. They also stressed courteous listening and quiet during meetings. In addition, they suggested asking members to refrain from describing food in detail during their speeches, because "descriptions of lists of foods or discussions of diets can be extremely disturbing to many members of the group."

Meanwhile, OA continued to grow. In April, 1961, a woman visted our Tuesday night meeting in West Los Angeles. Incredibly, she told us that her sister had started an Overeaters Anonymous group in Arizona, just outside of Phoenix. It turned out that the year before, at the same time Jo and I were starting OA in Los Angeles, Emma W. was beginning an identical group with the same name in Arizona. Excitedly I wrote to Emma, asking if her group would like to join with ours and the other two OA groups in California. Since both our programs followed AA's recovery program, we felt that in uniting ourselves, we would find greater strength. Much to our delight, Emma replied that they liked the idea, and with this union our Fellowship spread across the border of California.

Late in April three more groups sprang up. One was begun by Doreen in La Crescenta near Los Angeles. Doreen had been corresponding with us since seeing us on the Paul Coates show. She had started a weight-loss support group in February and wrote to us for information about OA. On April 19 we heard from her again:

> Dear Rozanne,
>
> Found your format most helpful. The group that I am asso-
> ciated with could not fully accept the OA Program (may I also
> add that it is as unsuccessful as you predicted), so I was most
> pleased when you sent me names of others who viewed your
> TV program and were interested.
>
> Called all those that had phones, and wrote to one who
> had no phone. . . . We set up our first meeting for last night,
> April 18th, at the Church of the Lighted Window in La
> Canada. . . .
>
> We don't know if you want names or not—but our first
> meeting was attended by five Compulsive Overeaters includ-
> ing myself. . . .

By this time Barbara's living room was bursting at the seams; every Tuesday night was standing room only. Many times we had to leave the front door open so that members could listen from the entry patio. It was obvious we would have to find another, more permanent place. After a flurry of phone calls, we finally settled on the auditorium at Temple Isaiah in West Los Angeles.

In early May a group was started in Long Beach, also near Los Angeles, and another was begun by Anne N. in Hayward, about forty miles south of San Francisco.

Two more groups began in June in the San Fernando Valley. Irene B., who had been attending since December 6, had become an enthusiastic member. By summer she had taken over from Mary L. as the contact person for the group meeting at the Panorama City playground on Friday mornings. At the same time, two other young women from the Valley, Darlene R., who had also been attending OA since December 6, and Betty R., who joined us in February, began an OA group in Van Nuys. These three Valley groups were destined to have a profound impact on OA in years to come.

Even after starting groups in the Valley, Irene and others continued driving over the hill for our West Los Angeles meeting on Tuesday nights. One summer night Irene offered to contact anybody who had written us from her area expressing an interest in OA. On July 22, I wrote to her:

Dear Irene,

According to our telephone conversation of July 21st, I'm enclosing the three sets of letters we discussed. . . . Please make our apologies to these people for making them wait so long for an answer. We've been explaining that there are only two or three of us answering the more than five hundred letters which we received as a result of the Paul Coates interview, and that we appreciated their patience.

Among the letters you will find the forms we asked them to return when they received our first letter in January. These people have already received the OA Program, so they will only need to be sent the Open Letter #2. All the others, however, who are writing in for the first time will need both the Open Letter #2 and the OA Program. . . . You (or perhaps it was Arvilla) mentioned at last week's meeting that you needed more OA Programs. We're running another thousand of them, and they should be ready in about 2 weeks. If you want any more, let us know.

As we also discussed on the phone, these letters are for you and Arvilla. Return them to me whenever you're finished with them.

Irene, thank you so much for your help in contacting these people. You've taken quite a load off of Myra's and my shoulders, for although it's a real joy to do this "Twelfth Step" work, the mail has gotten quite ahead of our ability to keep up with it.

Please let us know what happens with these people we're sending you, since we keep a record here in the General

Service Office of all contacts made and followed through. Also, please add to the list any groups you know of to which we could send people who write to us for help. . . . Love, Rozanne

In July Trudy L. started a Hollywood group, meeting Friday night at eight-thirty, and later another one at the same time on Thursday night. By this time we could see that we were going to need a directory of OA meeting times and places. When our first directory was printed on July 29, 1961, we listed fifteen OA groups—an amazing growth from the single group which had existed just six months before.

For the next six months the development of OA continued at a rapid pace. We discovered that, despite our efforts to give the new groups the benefit of our experience in West Los Angeles, they insisted on doing things their own way. As a result, they experienced many of the same growing pains we'd been through.

Meanwhile, we in the original group faced our first real controversy since the Paul Coates show. It seemed that the argument the summer before over whether or not to seek publicity was only a dress rehearsal for the disagreements still to come.

So far, we'd only had women in the meetings, but we'd had many letters from men inquiring about OA. Now the time had come to decide whether to open our groups to men.

I was in favor of welcoming all compulsive overeaters, regardless of gender. Barbara and several others, however, were adamantly opposed. Years later Barbara would say, "I felt there were intimate subjects of life that were personal, that I felt would be more appropriate to discuss with women and not to have men there. I also felt that men and women would be attracted to each other simply because some of the women were having difficult times at home, and this would be bad."

Feelings ran high, and we couldn't come to an agreement.

Finally we decided to set up a service board for the original Tuesday night group only. This board would meet separately from the meeting to deal with "the men problem" and other matters concerning the operation of the original group.

Barbara and I, along with six others, were the charter members of this board. Our first meeting was held in Barbara's living room on June 14, 1961.

OA had become very precious to all of us, and some members were afraid to take any action that would weaken our infant Fellowship. After a heated discussion, the majority on that fateful night ruled to close OA to men. They agreed that this would definitely apply to the Tuesday meeting, but some members decided to try to coax the other groups into agreement. These women also voted to close the Tuesday meeting to non-overeaters and to anyone under eighteen years old.

Recalling these vehement discussions, Roz B., another member who had joined right after the Paul Coates interview, would later reflect, "I remember OA during my first year as lots of arguing and me being a part of lots of arguing." The controversies that night were only the first of several OA would face in the coming months.

While I didn't agree with eliminating men from OA, I went along with the group conscience. Besides, I was still a practicing people-pleaser. Opting for peace at any price in order to hold OA together, I gave in when the vote went against my desires.

The establishment of this new service board to act as a steering committee for our original group marked a turning point for all of us. In taking this action, Barbara and I formally turned over leadership of the Tuesday night meeting, and by extension all of OA, to the group conscience. We both continued serving on the board for the next year, but no longer were we co-leaders for every meeting. Now, chosen by the committee, co-leaders rotated on a monthly basis.

Meanwhile, I was trying to juggle service work both within the original group and beyond it to our rapidly expanding Fellowship. Every night, after my husband and babies went to sleep, I worked until midnight corresponding with new groups and helping them get started, as well as trying to ease their growing pains.

In the late summer of 1961 Marvin and I traveled to the San Francisco area. There I met with Jean and other members of the Marin County group. The correspondence we exchanged after my visit shows clearly that face-to-face contact was a marvelous boost to everybody's spirits—especially mine.

A thank-you card signed by five members and received in September says it all:

"You were an inspiration to me!" wrote one woman. "I have had a most successful week & the spiritual guidance this week through constant reference to the Twelve Steps & prayer have been tremendous."

Jean's note was equally enthusiastic. "You have given us all renewed resolution and drive. Pounds are dropping all over the place, and we *feel wonderful.* Our warmest and deepest thanks, and best wishes to you and OA."

On October 10 I wrote back, adding my usual apologies and explanations for the delay in writing:

> Dear Jean and All You Wonderful Members of Marin OA,
>
> You have no idea how inspiring and heartwarming it was to receive your cards and notes. The only time OA is really meaningful is when the program brings results not only for oneself but for others as well. This is what AA calls "Twelfth Step Work," and it really does perpetuate this remarkable program for all time.
>
> It was a real pleasure to have met all of you, and I hope that whenever you're in Los Angeles, you'll do us the honor of attending one of our meetings, too. . . .
>
> I hope you are all still doing as well as your letters indicated. Have you been to an AA meeting yet? Have you bought AA's "Twelve Steps and Twelve Traditions" and "Just For Today"?

This letter includes the earliest mention of any OA tools,

although they are very different from the tools of recovery which later evolved for our Fellowship:

> Have you tried some of the "tools" we discussed, such as weighing and measuring of food, counting calories every day, keeping a weight and calorie chart, doing your grocery shopping right after a meal (on a full stomach) rather than just before a meal when you're hungriest? Remember also that we talked about "stripping" our homes of everything tempting to us. Children will benefit from lack of sweets, and we've found most husbands are cooperative when they see we really mean business. Watch out, too, for such excuses as buying food for the company that never drops in, or sweets for the children that they never get to see. Remember to plan ahead. This is one of the biggest pitfalls for the overeater, according to our collective experience. Whenever we don't have definite plans, particularly for family and individual menus, we have a tendency to grab and eat compulsively. Of course, this planning ahead applies to all areas of our lives. We have learned that whenever we're confused or rushed in any situation, we turn to food for relief. We've learned, too, that we overeat for no reason at all, or for any reason . . . such as frustration, boredom, stimulation, happiness, illness, good health, tragedy, good fortune, self-pity, jealousy, fear, guilt, etc. . . .
>
> By the way, all the "tools" I mentioned . . . are the result of our collective experience. Not every one is valid for every person, although most are effective to one degree or another. Anything that I or any other OA member may "recommend" is not an absolute "must" but merely a suggestion based on our experience in dealing with and overcoming our compulsive overeating. . . .
>
> Although I spoke much of the practical "tools," as we call them . . . don't forget the spiritual foundation on which this program is based. The simple spiritual truths of "Love Thy Neighbor," the practice of the Golden Rule, actions based on compassion, humility, gratitude . . . these are basic spiritual truths of which we speak. Sooner or later we begin to feel a need also for prayer and the surrender of our will (and willpower) to the care of a Power greater than ourselves.

(Whether this Power is a religious being, or a member of the group, or the group as a whole . . . the important thing is that we are asking for help from someone beyond ourselves.)

OA was growing rapidly. The path ahead seemed smooth and free from the bumps and potholes of life. For a brief period, we skipped down our road of happy destiny, blissfully unaware of the perilous curves ahead.

Chapter Four

The Spiritual-Psychological Controversy

LTHOUGH I would have been reluctant to admit it at first, Alcoholics Anonymous always had a tremendous impact on our Fellowship. Because of Jim W.'s urging, I attended AA meetings every week from early 1960 through 1969. In addition, local AA members spoke to us at our meetings for several years, teaching us the Twelve Steps and Twelve Traditions, helping us to understand their recovery program. These wonderful men and women gave of themselves unselfishly, and we owe them an enormous debt of gratitude.

After the Paul Coates show a number of women came to our meetings who were thoroughly familiar with AA's Twelve Steps. Some were AA members; others had family in AA. They introduced the AA philosophy into OA. Many were furious when they saw the changes I'd made in AA's original Steps, and they began agitating for OA to adopt the "real" AA Steps. No sooner had we settled the issue of not having men in OA than this new controversy entered our meetings. (Fortunately, we didn't know this pattern of arguing was to plague OA for years.)

One of the post-Coates-show women was Thelma S. from the Valley. Her husband had been in AA for sixteen years, and although she had a severe obesity problem, she understood the Steps and Traditions thoroughly. Once she found identification in OA, she was able to lose 110 pounds.

Thelma became my beloved sponsor. She saw beneath my self-willed exterior to what she called "the little girl inside of you." (That was thirty years before "the child within" became a catch phrase.) With Thelma's guidance, I began to work the Twelve Steps in earnest.

She took up my spiritual education where Jim had left off. Slowly she began to convince me of the value of surrender and dependence on a Higher Power. By late 1961 I was making some progress in that area. However, old habits die hard. Years later Hilda N. was to tell me, "You were opinionated, Rozanne. You always had a superior air, a patronizing air. But I'd never seen anybody so thin in my life. You oozed with success, and we wanted what you had."

My know-it-all attitude was both my undoing and the touchstone for my spiritual rebirth. At a meeting one night, a woman stood up and verbally attacked me in front of everyone. Another called me late at night a few days later and said some terrible things. Two nights later at ten o'clock she called and carried on again. I had no idea what I'd done to deserve such abuse. I can remember slamming down the phone, sobbing uncontrollably. I threw myself down on the floor of the darkened living room and cried out, "Okay, God, if you want me, you've got me." And that's how I finally surrendered and took Step Three.

My spiritual awakening was to directly affect what happened next in the OA Fellowship.

We earliest OA members had been atheists, agnostics and skeptics who strongly believed in the psychological basis for compulsive overeating. We had structured our program to de-emphasize the spiritual foundation of AA's Twelve-Step program. Now, suddenly I wanted to rewrite the OA Twelve Steps a third time, to make them like the AA Steps with their strong spiritual emphasis.

Many active members of our original Tuesday night group opposed OA's adopting the AA Steps exactly. They liked the psychological emphasis which OA had when they came in, and they felt that too much "God-talk" would drive away people who needed the program most.

The Spiritual-Psychological Controversy

Although I remained active in the Tuesday night group, I also visited those groups in the San Fernando Valley which strongly advocated the change to the AA Steps. These members argued vehemently that the power to recover came from a spiritual awakening. "The spiritual program," they insisted, "has worked for thousands of alcoholics in AA. It should form the basis of OA, too, or we'll be cheating ourselves and others of the real Power for recovery."

A great rift developed, and what we later called the "spiritual-psychological fight" began in earnest. It was a power struggle pitting most of the San Fernando Valley groups against the groups in Los Angeles. The Valley called Los Angeles the "psychology groups"; Los Angeles called the Valley the "Holy-Roller groups." Although there have always been differences in OA, this one was fundamental, and it was bitterly fought for six months.

Ethel K. and many of her group in Hollywood, as well as most of the Tuesday night board, felt strongly that the OA Steps should stay as they were. As the original group, we in West Los Angeles had been used to setting the OA standard for the offshoot meetings in the Valley and elsewhere. Now the "mother" group's supremacy was being threatened!

Irene B. carried the banner for change. "AA all the way," she cried. "These Steps are wrong!" Mildred J. and Darlene R. marched with her; soon many women in the Valley groups took up the charge. Irene and the others insisted that OA simply had to adopt the AA Twelve Steps, or they didn't want to be a part of us. Many of them looked to AA as a role model, rather than to us. They even started printing their own literature! Unbelievably, Irene and Mildred were agitating for withdrawal from OA in order to form their own organization.

A few Valley groups, which had been started by people from the parent group in Los Angeles, were either undecided or opposed to any change at all.

Phone lines heated up as calls went back and forth. Negative excitement caused many to return to food; others simply left OA. Looking back, it was our baptism by fire, but out of it came the OA that would survive and become a haven for thousands.

Talk of secession was everywhere; fear of OA destruction made us all feel very uneasy. Something had to be done.

In order to discuss this problem, a special agenda was called for the monthly board meeting of the Los Angeles parent group. On the last Wednesday in January, 1962, we met in my home. This was to be no usual meeting in any sense of the word. Feelings were at fever pitch that night, and running riot over everything was my own self-will.

I was distressed by the Valley groups' talk of disassociation, and I was equally unhappy with the Los Angeles groups' refusal to restore the Twelve Steps to their original AA wording. In my self-willed zeal, I tried to force upon the entire board my new spiritual awareness.

Unfortunately, I had neither the patience nor the compassion to understand that the others might have to reach such a point in their own good time. Hilda said, "If you want us to change, Rozanne, you have to give us time."

But I was impatient and stubborn. I can remember telling them, "If you and the group don't accept the spiritual side of things, then I'll take the OA name and the literature, and you all can go off and do things on your own!"

Hilda's jaw dropped; the others were equally stunned. In looking back, I can't imagine what I thought I'd do sitting alone in my dining room with a stack of literature and the name, Overeaters Anonymous.

There was a shocked and angry reaction to my ultimatum. When it finally died down, we began to discuss the situation. As we talked, we discovered we all had a common desire—we wanted OA to stay unified. After much discussion among ourselves that night and with the Valley groups later, a conference was called to attempt to resolve the matter. Small but potent, this was the first Overeaters Anonymous area conference, and it proved to be a turning point in the progress of OA.

The meeting took place on February 1, 1962. Nine

women represented six of the Los Angeles-San Fernando Valley groups. Irene B., Mable S., Thelma S., Sonny B. and Mildred J. were all there to speak for the Valley groups asking for change. Betty R. came for the Van Nuys meeting, the one Valley group holding out for the status quo. The groups insisting that the revised Steps remain had sent Ethel K. from Hollywood, Esther G. from Los Angeles and Lorraine Z. from the original Tuesday night group. I came to maintain strength for our General Service Office.

Years later Maxine R. would recall that Sonny was so exceptional because she could represent her group's viewpoint, yet not get angry and not fall apart. This was a time of great upheaval in OA, and serenity was truly an asset.

The discussion was heated that night. Irene and Mildred talked of pulling their groups out of OA, adopting another name and printing new literature which would incorporate the Steps as AA had written them. Thelma, Mable and Sonny took a more moderate viewpoint. They agreed that the Steps should be changed to the AA version, but they favored remaining with OA. Ethel, Esther and Betty stubbornly clung to the current OA Steps, refusing to compromise.

My heart sank as I sat there listening to the words swirl around me. I thought about that awful year of 1959, after my first visit to Gamblers Anonymous, when I had struggled hopelessly with my disease. Remembering my search for the kind of fellowship I'd experienced at GA, I recalled what I'd said to myself at the first glimmer of my new idea. "Someday OA will be as big as AA, or bigger, and it will be all around the world." I believed that no overeater who had suffered as I had would ever have to cry out for help in vain. Yet now, just when OA was beginning to grow and spread, it all seemed to be falling apart.

At this point I was willing to accept the Twelve Steps exactly as AA had written them. "From my experience," I said to the others, "the watered-down Steps are not as effective as they might be. Your groups which use them might at least try the suggested changes." My firm belief was in unity at any cost.

Ethel, whose voice was deep and loud, overreacted. Esther, with an equally strong voice, jumped into the fray, refusing to budge. That provoked the others, and confusion filled the room.

Suddenly, everything stopped. We had a born mediator in our midst, and quietly she took control. Lorraine had a soft voice and a happy smile, and it was she who saved the day. She stood up in front of all of us and said, "Please girls, let's be reasonable. Our main disagreement seems to be how we are going to print the Steps in our literature. You know, each group is autonomous and can do what it wants, but our literature should show a unified foundation. Therefore," she went on, "let's revise our Twelve Steps to read exactly like AA's Steps. We'll print new literature with the rewritten Steps, the only substitutions being 'food' for 'alcohol' and 'compulsive overeater' for 'alcoholic.' Each group will still be free to interpret them and do what it wants." Still smiling sweetly, she sat down.

The eight women looked at one another. I held my breath. After more discussion, everyone agreed to accept this compromise. It left groups and individuals free to interpret the program as they saw fit, yet we would have unity in the literature and a firm basis for growth in the Steps.

Now we had weathered two major disagreements—whether to allow men in OA and the spiritual-psychological differences—and it seemed as if we had become stronger in the process.

But these were just local groups; I envisioned something grander. My father had been Executive Secretary of a B'nai B'rith District, which had encompassed eight midwestern states and part of Canada. One of his primary functions was creating, planning and coordinating conventions and business conferences throughout his large district. My parents often discussed these gatherings at home, and I had grown up learning the value of organizational get-togethers and how to bring them about.

With this background, it was only natural for me to suggest at that February, 1962, meeting, "Let's have a conference of all the OA groups! We could send out a letter to each group inviting them to send a representative."

As scary as it was, this little mini-conference, born out of crisis, showed us the power of unity. After more talk, the vote was unanimous. We would have a true Overeaters Anonymous Conference to be held annually in Los Angeles.

I was assigned to write a notice about our plans to all group secretaries and leaders. It was the first attempt to bring our struggling groups together, and it proved to be a major step in fostering OA communication and unity.

I gave my assignment a great deal of thought. How could we most effectively bind ourselves into a cohesive organization through the written word? This notice was important, since it was to include not only the idea of a conference but other OA news as well. Finally, in early May, 1962, we published the first issue of a brand-new publication, the *OA Bulletin*. This little three-page newsletter was the forerunner of the *OA Lifeline*, a publication designed to share information and experience throughout the Fellowship. The first issue of the *Bulletin* was addressed to OA's sixteen groups (which were listed along with their contact people at the top of the front page), "and to all other secretaries and leaders of Overeaters Anonymous."

> Hi, everyone! This is our very first OA bulletin. It's also a letter serving to introduce you to one another . . . and to let all of you know that you have joined hands with at least 200 OA members in helping each other to stop eating compulsively and to maintain a normal weight.
>
> If we have overlooked or omitted any name from the list above, please forgive us. That's really the main purpose of this letter-bulletin. We don't know much about what many of the other groups are doing; in many cases we don't even know the names of the secretaries.

We enclosed our first and only meeting directory, dated July, 1961, which listed fifteen groups. Then we asked for corrections and other changes for our second directory to be published at the end of May. After making specific requests, the *Bulletin* went on:

> And oh, how important this Directory is! Try, if you can, to remember back to the time when you were drowning in a sea of compulsion and were desperate for help. You didn't know where to turn . . . no number listed in the phone book, no help from any quarter. Suddenly, mercifully, you heard about Overeaters Anonymous.
>
> Perhaps you saw a small notice in your local paper, perhaps you watched that fateful Paul Coates show late in 1960, perhaps a friend mentioned OA to you, or a doctor or minister referred you to us. At last you had found a haven of understanding, help and hope. There are hundreds of thousands just like you . . . and now, when they write to us here at the Beverly Hills P.O. Box number, we can send them a list of groups; immediate help so that they too can make their lives more manageable at last.
>
> In view of this, we know you'll recognize the importance of sending us the proper information for this Directory and for keeping us informed in the future of any changes or additional groups being formed.

There were some personal notes in that first *Bulletin*:

> Anne, your letters and Marion's telling us of your astounding weight losses and spiritual progress both personally and group-wise have been most inspiring. Emma, your news about the new groups in Mesa, Mojave and the East was very exciting. Can you tell us more about them? You really have some wonderful "Twelfth Step" workers in your group!

News concerning the February 1 meeting carried no hint of the controversy which had surrounded it:

> More exciting news! On February 1st of this year we had our first informal (and very impromptu) OA Conference. It was made up of secretaries and General Service Office representatives from six of the groups surrounding the Los Angeles area and Rozanne S. representing the General Service Office. At that meeting we talked of many things concerning OA. The only definite thing that came out of it was a determination to unify all the groups into a loosely-knit fellowship, precisely as

AA has done. Also, it was decided that the time had come for a revision and strengthening of our four-page Program. Therefore, in about three months you'll all receive a copy of the new material. Most of it is being adapted directly from the Alcoholics Anonymous literature, since our Program is based wholly upon theirs. Also, our Twelve Steps and Twelve Unifying Rules will be re-written to correspond exactly to theirs, with the substitution of "compulsive overeating" for "alcoholism" wherever necessary. Since this is *your* fellowship, any ideas or comments on the above will be appreciated.

Then we announced an idea that would have a tremendous impact on OA's future:

Also, out of the "Conference" came a very real desire to have a true "Overeaters Anonymous Conference" held annually here in Los Angeles. It would be made up of representatives from all OA groups across the country. This is just in the talking stage right now . . . let us know your opinions.

We also made an "SOS" appeal to all OA groups to support the General Service Office in the form of monthly voluntary contributions.

Finally, for the first time in our literature I wrote about an idea recently introduced to OA, a subject which was to have a permanent effect on Overeaters Anonymous—the concept of "Abstinence." (This early introduction appears in full in Chapter Eleven.)

Our first *Bulletin* ended with a paragraph promising, "We will be sending you periodic bulletins from now on. . . . Please let us hear from you."

By the time the *Bulletin* was mailed out, I was already busy revising our original four-page piece of literature in order to restore the Twelve Steps and change our Twelve Unifying Rules. Now our revised Twelve Steps and Twelve Traditions would be essentially identical to those of AA. By making these adjustments, we would strengthen the spiritual basis of the OA program and achieve unity for our Fellowship. In addition, we'd had a few more committee meetings and decided to hold our first OA Conference in Los Angeles on August 11 and 12, 1962.

Early in June I mailed *Conference Bulletin #1* to all OA groups and group secretaries. The first paragraph read:

> This is really an exciting period in the growth of Overeaters Anonymous! As you can see from the enclosed notice, we are planning our first National Conference. This is a result of the response from your letters, which indicated a real need for unifying all the O.A. groups into what A.A. calls a "loosely-knit Fellowship."

We followed with a list of the items to be discussed: literature, our General Service Office and whether we were ready to handle national publicity.

In the midst of all this flurry, Marvin and I took our children to visit my brother and his family in Albuquerque, New Mexico for two weeks. This family reunion provided me with a much-needed vacation from all my OA activity. It was the last such relief I was to experience for another year.

The first thing I did upon our return (after unpacking, laundry and child care, of course) was to write and mail *Conference Bulletin #2*. During our absence, replies to our first mailing had been coming in, so this *Bulletin* began:

> TO ALL DELEGATES TO THE FIRST
> NATIONAL OA CONFERENCE:
> Your response to our first conference bulletin has been very heartwarming and inspiring! It now looks as though there will finally be some unified help for compulsive overeaters, just as there is for alcoholics! Of course, Overeaters Anonymous is small and is still having growing pains, but our path to recovery is clear and our O.A.-A.A. Program has proven itself successful beyond a doubt to those who earnestly try.

After two pages of remarks to various members and specific Conference information, the *Bulletin* ended on a hopeful note:

> This National Conference is a big step for all of us in Overeaters Anonymous. It represents the second and third of the three legacies handed to us by Alcoholics Anonymous— Recovery, Unity, Service. Recovery for each of us as individ-

uals, Unity for all of us as groups, and Service *to* all of us by our trusted members as our elected representatives. The Conference means also that in unity Overeaters Anonymous will exist to help us maintain our own recovery and to carry the message to the compulsive overeater who still suffers.

In the meantime, between our first little February area conference and the mailing of the *Bulletin* in May, I'd been working on a major project. It was to be a new forty-page book for OA. I was determined to adapt AA literature wherever possible for use in OA instead of writing something new. As a result, I decided to adapt the first portion of AA's "Big Book," *Alcoholics Anonymous.* I used many passages word for word, making appropriate changes for compulsive overeating and the overeater whenever the book referred to alcoholism and the alcoholic. In addition, I wrote an original chapter entitled "The Overeater, The Alcoholic, and The Gambler." In it I described in great detail the behavior of the compulsive overeater, and briefly described the similarities between the three diseases. The chapter ended with the following paragraph:

> We are humbly thankful to God, as we each understand Him, for showing us the way in which we can join with others to control our life-destroying compulsion. We hope that in unity—Overeaters Anonymous, Alcoholics Anonymous, Gamblers Anonymous and all other fellowships like them, joined by medicine, psychiatry and religion—we can shed light on the darkness of our suffering and help others as we have been helped ourselves.

Oh, I was so proud of that little book, especially my last chapter. Excitedly, on June 9, 1962, I wrote AA's General Service Office in New York, enclosing a copy of our proposed new publication:

> Dear Miss M_____:
>   . . . We have suggested to our members that they read the book "Alcoholics Anonymous". We have also told them how much we have benefited from all the AA literature. We feel that your AA book is truly remarkable and inspired. We are

sure that we couldn't say what must be said nearly as well as it is done in this book.

Therefore, we would like to use excerpts from it in our new booklet. . . . We hope we may have the permission of the proper AA committee for the use of the many passages from "Alcoholics Anonymous". . . .

On July 20, 1962, Herbert A. Morse, the non-AA Chairman of AA's General Service Board, responded to my letter:

Dear Miss S_____:

Thank you for your letter asking permission to use excerpts from our book "Alcoholics Anonymous" in a booklet for your organization. We are flattered that you put so much value on our expression of the A.A. recovery program.

We have read your manuscript and feel that if we granted permission for the use of the material from our book it would be a violation of our copyright which would affect us in the near future. Regretfully, therefore, we must deny you permission to use our material.

We have no objection to sharing the ideas in our book provided you wished to put the ideas into your own words.

We are sorry to have been of so little help. Best wishes and success in your program to help others.

When I read that letter, I was crushed! I had worked so hard on that book; was all that effort for nothing? Our first OA Conference was just a month away, and we had expected to have the material ready to present to that historic gathering. Now we'd have to start all over, and this time we'd have to carefully avoid the use of direct quotes from the "Big Book" and AA's "Twelve and Twelve."

I wondered: Could we ever write anything that would win approval of both the spiritual and psychological factions in OA? Well, there was no time for regrets. It was mid-July, and I had all I could do to get ready for the Conference, which was just around the corner.

Our excitement mounted as group responses continued to come in to our post office box. We could see that there would be representatives from nearly all OA groups, an incredible happening for an organization which only two years before had consisted of just two young women.

Our young Fellowship had grown far beyond Los Angeles. We had weathered our first controversies, begun to publish our own literature on a regular basis, extended the hand of fellowship and hope to hundreds of suffering compulsive overeaters. Many were now committed to OA, had begun to work the Twelve Steps and had a taste of recovery. For all of us, OA recovery opened up a new world of friendship, support and hope, filling us with an unquenchable enthusiasm. It's hard to put into words the excitement of those early years. I was obsessed, totally obsessed for years with OA, and so were many who joined me.

Bernice S. would later say, "I needed that togetherness that we have and that strong bond. We ladies in the Valley were very, very tight. It was great."

Maxine R., who joined in September of 1961, remembered her experience during her first year: "I had this feeling that we were kind of like the blind leading the blind, but we all knew it was okay. I didn't understand the Steps and I didn't understand what was going on, but I understood the Fellowship. I understood that people were willing to call each other, which was very nice. It was the first time I was able to share with other people on an emotional basis what was going on with me. I had tried many things and none of them had worked, and I always had the feeling that I was the only one who ever ate that way. When I heard people sharing at the meetings about the way they were eating, which was a lot the way I was eating, that made me feel that I was not a freak, and I was not alone."

Nicky was another old-timer who recalled, "I was so impressed with OA because of the friendship," and her sentiments were echoed by Charlotte, who added, "It was so good for me to feel that I had something that I could go to that was for me, that I could use in living."

Zelda T., who joined OA in June of 1962 and very quickly became involved in service, reflected on the early OA spirit:

"The first year was like coming out to the top of the mountain and finding answers I had never been able to find. And I found identification with so many people. It was like a love affair. For the first time in my life I fell in love with something, and it was OA and the people in OA. I identified and I envied everybody in OA, and I kept saying, 'If they can do it, I can do it.'

"It was the happiest time of my life, when I first came to OA. And it's been the best adventure I've ever had."

These women summed up our incredible summer of 1962. Much had gone before, much lay ahead. We could only walk together into the future with the belief that we were the carriers of a magnificent message of faith, hope and recovery.

Chapter Five

Male Call!

EMEMBER the gender-related discussions we had in early 1961? Because of the "delicate" nature of our talks in meetings, the majority of members in the original group had voted to close OA to men. Ours was to be a women-only Fellowship. Now fate intervened, and all that was about to change!

While I'd been vacationing in Albuquerque, a man from Texas had come through Los Angeles on his way to the Seattle World's Fair with his family. He'd called my home looking for OA, and when no one answered, he called the local AA office and left his phone number and address, asking me to contact him in Texas.

A.G.A. (everyone called him "A.G.") was a fascinating man, a successful businessman in the petroleum industry. He was also, by his own account, ". . . fully qualified as a compulsive eater. Most of my life I'd weighed more than three hundred pounds."

In May of 1961, A.G. had an experience which changed his life, and he talked about it freely: "I was a very fat thirty-one-year-old, riding in a car with two other men from a church meeting in West Texas. One of the other men in the car [John B.] was an alcoholic with slightly more than two years of sobriety in AA. I finally got up the courage to ask John if he thought the AA program could do anything to help someone like me. He paused a long time, thinking about my question. Then he nodded his head and said, 'I don't see why not.'

"I didn't know much about the Twelve Steps, but God made it possible for me at that moment to understand that John wanted to drink for the same reasons that I wanted to eat, and that if something had made it possible for him to avoid that for over two years, by God, maybe I could, too.

"In the next twenty-four hours, I had an overwhelming spiritual experience that has changed my life every minute— abstinent or not—from that day to this one.

"[Then] John went to his regular AA meetings in this area of small-town Texas and told them about me. Each group voted to accept me at all meetings, both open and closed. My appreciation knows no bounds for their open-mindedness, compassion and acceptance of someone suffering from another compulsion."

A.G. began attending AA meetings and retreats near his hometown of Luling, Texas. Thirty-four days after his spiritual experience, he made his first Twelfth-Step call on Norma B., a long-time friend and fellow compulsive overeater. When Norma agreed to join A.G. in his endeavors, the local AA groups also welcomed her at all their meetings.

In 1961, with John's help, Norma and A.G. formed Gluttons Anonymous, based on AA's Twelve Steps and Twelve Traditions. A.G. and Norma lost their excess weight, and within two years Gluttons Anonymous had grown to five Texas groups in Austin, San Antonio and Luling.

Although Gluttons Anonymous followed AA's program, A.G remembers that the Texas meetings had one added feature:

"We came in and we wrote our weight down. We decided it had been too long since we had told anyone, including ourselves, the truth about our weight. . . . That was sort of a cleansing act in and of itself.

"We didn't have the term 'abstinence.' We called it sobriety, and we spoke about our diet. Early Gluttons Anonymous meetings were just like AA meetings, and alcoholics came to our meetings to help us learn the program. There was no controversy because we were simply trying to do exactly what AAs did to recover, and it was working."

A.G.'s success in using a Twelve-Step program to recover from compulsive overeating led him to wonder if there might be other groups in other places doing the same thing. Exploring the possibilities, he wrote to AA's General Service Office in New York City.

Several months after the Paul Coates telecast, I had written to that same office telling them about us and offering our office number (still in my dining room) for anyone who might be interested. Therefore, when A.G.'s letter arrived, they simply forwarded our information to him.

Shortly after we returned from our vacation, the local AA service office called to tell me of his inquiry. On July 11, 1962, I wrote to him. Not knowing about Gluttons Anonymous, I assumed he was a compulsive overeater wanting information about OA. How could I know that this mysterious Texan would soon be our first male member and chairman of OA's first Board of Trustees?

I sent him our four-page booklet, a current meeting directory, the Serenity Prayer, our little two-page *Just For Today* and a small pamphlet called *Fifteen Points To Keep In Mind Before You Take That First Bite.*

I also encouraged him to start an OA group for himself and to visit local AA meetings.

Perhaps most important, I described our upcoming National Conference and sent him a copy of our proposed forty-page book.

Unaware of the changes about to burst upon the OA scene, I filed that letter and busied myself with the upcoming Conference. Of course, I still took care of my home and husband, as well as six-year-old Debbie and four-and-a-half-year-old Julie. That was definitely a hectic summer at my house!

July 15, 1962, was my thirty-third birthday. In the midst of a family celebration, the OA phone rang. "Who's calling on a Sunday night?" I asked as I ran to answer.

I picked up the phone; my life changed and OA's future abruptly took a new direction.

The voice on the other end had an unmistakable Texas twang. "Rozanne, this is A.G.," he said. "I received your letter, and I'm calling from our Sunday night Gluttons Anonymous meeting. We have five groups here in Texas, and we're interested in hearing more about your OA."

I was very excited, although I certainly tried not to show it on the phone. Motioning to Marvin to take over the kids and the kitchen, I carried on with the conversation. A.G. described Gluttons Anonymous, I described OA, and then I told him about our upcoming National Conference. Plunging ahead, I invited him to consider bringing his five groups into OA. With sixteen groups, we were a larger organization. "Just a minute," he answered. I heard voices in the background; my heart was pounding. It took a few minutes, then he was back on the phone.

"Rozanne," he drawled, "we've just had a little meeting, and we want to accept your invitation. We're interested in affiliating with OA. We'll be bringing several delegates from our groups, plus some wives, and I'll be flying all of us in with my private airplane." I was dazzled! A Texas "oilman" winging in for our Conference!

Hanging up the phone, I was beside myself with excitement. Then suddenly it dawned on me. Only the year before, the West Los Angeles board had voted "no men in OA." Now I'd taken it upon myself to invite a man, perhaps more than one, to the Conference. What should I do?

Well, it was obvious; there was only one thing I could do. I called the Conference committee right away. Barbara had left OA by this time, and most of the people who had objected to men were no longer with us. "You'll never guess what happened," I told the committee members. As I related the story, they were all delighted at the prospect and voted unanimously to invite him and any other Texas delegates to attend the Conference.

(During the World Service Convention in Minneapolis in 1995, A.G. would relate his view of this story. "I'm sure there were other men out there trying to get in," he would laugh. "I just happened to be first in line when they opened the door and let us in.")

I was pleased with the results of the vote. At last we

would have a gender-balanced membership in Overeaters Anonymous! Not only would he be the first man in OA, but A.G. was to have a major influence on our development as well.

I still treasure the letter A.G. wrote to me after that call:

July 16, 1962

Dear Rozanne,

I hope you know how pleased we all were to make contact with you and the other groups last night. We are all on Cloud 9 today. We have made many other attempts to contact other groups, including writing the General Services Council of AA in New York, but never got any results before. We had eagerly checked the mail every day since I returned from Los Angeles hoping to hear from you.

I am enclosing a copy of our preamble and a copy of our questionnaire for prospective members which might be of some help in writing something for use in all the groups. . . .

We are looking forward to meeting you in August at the convention. My sponsor and I will attend, probably with our wives, and we hope that two other members will accompany us.

Let us know what you think of this material and send us any convention information you may have available.

Very sincerely yours, A.G.

I immediately wrote back to A.G.:

July 19, 1962

Dear A.G.,

We are all just as happy and excited as you are at the affiliation of your groups with Overeaters Anonymous. We are convinced, as I'm sure you are, too, that only in widespread unity can this program of recovery be offered to all suffering overeaters everywhere. This is the eventuality for which we are striving. It may be many, many years off, but it will come in time.

You'll notice that I said that this program will be offered to overeaters everywhere. Acceptance of it is another problem, and I imagine our percentage of true recovery is about the same as yours. However, we are finding the percentage slow-ly rising, especially in the last year. Perhaps it is because of the spreading knowledge that OA is no mere diet-and-exer-cise club, but a place where the truly desperate can recover from a progressive illness if they are willing and honest.

We, also, are all looking forward to meeting you at the Conference. It promises to be an exciting and rewarding time for all of us.

After including information about airport and hotel arrangements, I added:

I'm taking your material to the meeting today, and I'm sure they'll all like it as much as I did. . . .

We are eagerly awaiting your next letter and are looking forward to your arrival on August 10!

Sincerely,

Rozanne S. for Overeaters Anonymous

"Eagerly awaiting" was an understatement. Most of us were homemakers with small children; all of us were im-pressed with A.G.'s proposed mode of transportation. "Just imagine," we exulted to one another, "a private plane!"

Although we didn't recognize it that July, A.G.'s business expertise was to dramatically affect OA's corporate affairs in a very positive manner.

Back at my home front, I was juggling home responsibil-ities, husband and child care, OA office work, nonstop tele-phone calls and arrangements for the upcoming Conference. By mid-August I weighed 103 pounds and wore a size six. My body finally looked the way I had always dreamed it would (although most of my emotional and spiritual recovery still lay ahead).

Chapter Six

A Meeting of the Minds

UDDENLY, it was Saturday, August 11, 1962—the day of our first National OA Conference. I was partly numb, partly overwhelmed with antici-pation. The Conference was scheduled at the Bel Air Sands Hotel in West Los Angeles. We were to start at 9:15 in the morn-ing and continue until 5:30, with the usual lunch break. Then we planned to meet on Sunday morning from 9:15 until noon.

As an added event, we scheduled an Open Conference Sunday afternoon at the American Legion Hall in Los Angeles. This would be the forerunner of our OA Conventions, where delegates and other members would share their stories of re-covery.

We could all feel the excitement in the air that Saturday morning. Would this be the beginning of a unified Fellowship? Could we pull ourselves together and fulfill the promise of the First Tradition? We all sensed that we were present at a signifi-cant moment in OA's growth.

Fifteen delegates from OA's twenty-one groups gathered at the hotel on Sunset Boulevard for our opening meeting. Having lost more than one hundred pounds, A.G. turned out to be the very image of the tall, handsome Texan. As promised, he'd ar-rived in Los Angeles piloting his private plane, a light, twin Piper Aztec. He was accompanied by his friend and sponsor, John B., their wives, and the Gluttons Anonymous cofounder, Norma B.

Laughing and chatting as we all gathered in the conference room were Jean R. and Maureen from Northern California, and Emma W. representing the Arizona groups in Phoenix, Tempe and Mesa. A.G., representing Luling, Texas, and Norma B., representing Austin, Texas, smiled and introduced themselves to the women from Southern California. Bea R. from North Hollywood, Irene B. from Sun Valley, Mildred J. from Sunland, Sonny B. from Tarzana, Thelma S. from Panorama City and Mabel S. from Pacoima made up the delegates from the San Fernando Valley. The rest of Los Angeles sent Carol G. of Lennox, Ethel K. of Hollywood, Fran S. of Torrance and Lorraine Z. from the original West Los Angeles group. I represented the OA General Service Office and would chair the meeting.

Three decades later, A.G. would reminisce: "Going out to California was a real experience. It's hard to express the joy I felt to be in a room with maybe fifty or sixty people who were like I was. It was a big deal. The spirit of God was certainly evident there."

As the clock moved towards 9:15, everyone took a seat. The happy talking stopped, the room became very quiet and everyone looked at me with anticipation.

I took a deep breath, stood up slowly and said, "Good morning, my friends. My name is Rozanne, and I'm a compulsive overeater." "Hi, Rozanne," they all responded warmly.

Trembling inside, I looked out at all those expectant faces and plunged onward. "Welcome to the very first National Conference of Overeaters Anonymous. Would you all join me in the Serenity Prayer."

During our recitation, I was both moved and excited by the prospect of what we had set in motion. My original dream of a worldwide Fellowship seemed poised on the brink of reality!

"Will you please read the Twelve Steps," I smiled at one of the delegates. As she spoke, I could see intense concentration on the faces of the assembled members.

Next, I asked each delegate to stand, introduce herself

and tell us what group she represented. After the women had finished, I talked about our "no men" vote of the year before, the phone call of the previous month—and then I introduced "our first male member, A.G. from Luling, Texas." The audience burst into enthusiastic applause, and the room filled with welcoming warmth. I let out my breath; it was an encouraging start.

Following the introductions, another woman came up to the front and stated our Twelve Traditions. Then I read aloud our agenda for the Conference. Thankfully, everyone was still quiet—waiting. The real test lay ahead.

"And now let's move on to the first order of business," I continued, "which is our proposed OA literature."

We began with a discussion about an introductory pamphlet. This would be sent to people inquiring about OA and would also be sold at meetings. It was to be sixteen pages, narrow and long to fit into a business-size envelope. It would introduce the OA program, define the terms we used and answer many other questions. It would also include the Twelve Steps, Twelve Traditions and the Serenity Prayer.

After much discussion, the delegates voted unanimously in favor of this booklet. I was asked to create a pamphlet fulfilling the various objectives. This turned out to be our very first totally original piece of literature, and it was entitled *Questions and Answers About Compulsive Overeating and the OA Recovery Program.*

Next on the agenda was a trilogy of pamphlets: *Just For Today, Fifteen Points to Keep in Mind Before You Take That First Bite* and *If God Spoke To OA, He Might Have Said . . . .*

Sometime during 1961 Irene had found these three pieces of literature at her local AA meetings. She brought them back to be reprinted by the Valley groups. When I called the Los Angeles AA Central Service Office to inquire about them, the secretary told me that these pamphlets had been written by some local AA members and published without a copyright notice. A few months earlier, when I had "borrowed" a portion of AA's "Big Book," I had rewritten various parts of it for the compulsive overeater. (Naively, I believed that wasn't a copyright violation.) However, I strenuously objected to simply reprinting outside literature as our own.

But Irene was absolutely adamant. She found a printer and began reproducing these three pieces for "her" Valley meetings. "If local groups want to print their particular choice [of literature]," she said, "then if it's great, it will spread all over the country." She was stubborn, and her attitude infuriated me.

That's how matters stood when the delegates turned their attention to the first of Irene's three proposed booklets, *Just For Today*. At first the discussion was friendly and the vote was unanimous. We all liked *Just For Today*, although it was not written by us, so this little essay became our second piece of OA literature.

The next pamphlet we discussed was also adapted from local AA material. It was called *Fifteen Points To Keep in Mind Before You Take That First Bite*. There was general agreement that this needed rewriting, so a committee comprised of Irene, Ethel, Lorraine and me was formed to take care of the matter. Up to this point, the meeting had been surprisingly harmonious, but the harmony was about to end.

Remember the local area meeting six months earlier? That February argument between the "spiritual Valley groups" and the "psychological Los Angeles groups" had centered on bringing our revised Twelve Steps into line with AA's Steps.

At that time the Valley groups had clamored for "pure" AA Steps. The Los Angeles groups had insisted on keeping our rewritten Steps as they were.

Since that time there had been a subtle shift in the battleground of the two warring factions. The Valley purists had gotten their way on the issue of the Steps, but they were still unhappy. They now insisted that OA should be a totally spiritual program, and they wanted our literature to reflect that fact. If they didn't get their way, some of those members talked of breaking away and forming their own organization.

In the meantime, those Los Angeles members who had

wanted to keep the originally-revised OA Steps and empha-size the psychological aspect had also changed. They were now strongly advocating that our literature reflect a balanced program consisting of three parts—spiritual, emotional and physical.

The two factions, which had been warring for almost a year, seemed to have reached a point where they no longer listened to each other. Almost every delegate from the Los Angeles-Valley area seemed to have made up her mind ahead of time which side she would support.

Meanwhile, the Northern California, Arizona and Texas delegates had no idea that a conflict existed. They were about to be taken by surprise by the vehemence of the local delegates, as we all discussed the rest of the issues facing the Conference. I could only hope and pray that OA would stay together for everyone's sake.

All these dynamics came into play as we began to discuss the last pamphlet in Irene's trilogy, entitled *If God Spoke to OA He Might Have Said* . . . . Nine delegates had voiced their approval of the pamphlet when Lorraine stood up to oppose it. Lorraine, who was donating many hours to print OA liter-ature at cost in her family-owned print shop, cared deeply about the message OA literature carried. She disliked *If God Spoke* . . . because it emphasized only the spiritual aspect of the program. "Our literature," she said, "should reflect that there are three aspects to OA: spiritual, psychological and physical."

Thelma had a strong spiritual program and years of ex-posure to the Twelve Steps and Twelve Traditions through her husband's AA membership. She objected to the pam-phlet's phrase, "priests and ministers." She felt this tied it to a particular religion.

Then Ethel joined in, and I could feel the tension rising in the room as her deep, deliberate voice commanded every-one's attention. Ethel had been so well-known in OA as a proponent of psychological recovery that no one in the room realized she had shifted her position. Now she began talking about all three elements of recovery—spiritual, emotional and physical.

"We consider that OA has three factors that are vitally concerned here," she began. "We, perhaps more than some of the other groups, believe that the psychological, or emotional if you wish to call it that, is . . . vital. My primary interest is that a new group, or a potential group, should receive from OA a balanced, representative amount of literature. . . . Now, is it going to be the Twelve Steps and the Twelve Traditions, which we all agreed is basic, and then on top of that, is it *all* going to be a prayer . . . or is there really going to be on the part of this group an attempt to establish more general literature, also in these other fields? . . . Now I tell you that if this group only promulgates literature that I choose to call religious . . . and nothing else, then I know that our group will be very disturbed. . . . The only thing I would like is that we put some equal amount of effort into getting our program based on three things instead of just on one."

Lorraine had been our peacemaker at the February meeting. When she got up again to state her group's point of view, I hoped she would play the same role now. As she spoke, however, it was clear that she would not compromise on the pamphlet under discussion.

"At the West Los Angeles OA group," she said, "it was requested that we develop a program [that] didn't lean. They feel that it's tilting more to one side, and they would prefer getting . . . three phases of the program for people who have come in to effect a change in their eating habits. . . . If people feel that [this pamphlet] would be wanted in such quantities, that's fine; perhaps our group may want it in larger quantities than any, but also they might want in equally large quantities different types of literature that encompass the other two facets of our program."

Confused, A.G. asked Ethel and Lorraine to explain specifically what they meant by "other types of literature." The two women suggested literature on the mechanics or "tools" of abstinence—specifically, stripping the house, not buying food for company that never comes and suggesting that the newcomer read related literature.

Because Jean R. was from Northern California, she had not been involved in the controversy of the past year. Therefore, she had trouble understanding why Ethel and Lorraine had such strong objections. "I like the 'three-phase' aspect of our program, too," she said. "However, we are considering a specific piece of literature. There has been nothing printed on the physical or emotional side, and I think that should be considered when something has been submitted. I don't think this [*If God Spoke* . . . pamphlet] should crowd it out, but how can we discuss . . . [any other pamphlet] if it isn't here?"

Emma from Arizona was frightened by the anger in people's voices and the veiled threats to leave OA. "I would like to see literature on the tools, too," she said. "But for now, let's take what we have. We can add other kinds of pamphlets later. And for goodness sake, let's not separate!"

Irene wouldn't give up. This pamphlet was her baby! She stood to speak in favor of it and against Ethel's and Lorraine's calls for a three-sided program. "The program is mostly spiritual," she exclaimed. "In fact, it [the spiritual] is the *only* side. If a group is interested in the psychological . . . what's wrong with a group printing it themselves? If it's the real message, it'll go all over. Nothing can stop it."

Bea was more practical. "If the demand is great enough, then it's cheaper to have it printed centrally. This is also true of other literature."

Ethel spoke again, becoming more defiant as she gathered steam. "The crux of the problem with this pamphlet is that it is religious rather than spiritual. I urge you again to try and broaden your view to the concept of 'God as we understand Him.' Now, this is my objection to this pamphlet. It limits the concept of God. If we print it, we should at least change 'priests and ministers' and change 'He might have said . . .' to wording that is less restrictive."

Lorraine added, "OA is not a religion. . . . Some people lost their weight in OA before there was a spiritual concept. . . . They used the physical, psychological, the power of the group . . . before they added the spiritual concept. There are many ways of a group acting together to instill this wonderful feeling of success, and everybody understands the spiritual aspect in their own way."

Then she held up a copy of the four-page brochure which I had written right after the Paul Coates show as an example of OA literature which presented a more balanced program, especially for newcomers. "This piece of paper," Lorraine went on, "says we're powerless, we should come to meetings regularly. This talks about the basic facts to people. This is what I'm looking for."

At that point I stood up to explain that the proposed *Questions and Answers* booklet was intended to explain the program to newcomers and present the tools, as had my original four-page booklet.

Ironically, it was Ethel who finally gave up on further discussion and said, "Let's take a vote on printing *If God Spoke to OA, He Might Have Said* . . . . Our little group voted eleven to four to print it, with the provision that the phrase 'priests and ministers' be changed to 'spiritual leaders.'" There was applause as we all breathed a sigh of relief. It was the lull before the storm.

The next topic to be discussed was OA itself. This was a fundamental subject: What is OA? What is our basic philosophy? If we couldn't agree on this, our Fellowship could not survive. If we could find mutual understanding, it would form the bedrock foundation upon which we could begin to build OA both as an organization and as a Fellowship.

In order to understand how Overeaters Anonymous established a basis for unity, imagine yourself back in that meeting hall on a warm August afternoon. Everyone is quiet, listening intently. Ethel is speaking:

"At a preparatory meeting for this Conference, I was told that there is only one way (I am paraphrasing), that certain groups have *the* way to accomplish our mutual purpose, and no other way is right. Now this was very difficult for me to accept, and I go on record as saying I do not . . . and I say 'I' meaning my group . . . we do not accept this. Rozanne has just said that no OA group has *the* way, no OA group has *the* power, sanely, to judge any other OA group, that we are all OA as long as we do not violate the rules of OA, which are quite simple, and they are not confining."

Her voice was strong as she went on. "I wish to know whether this Conference endorses Rozanne's statement of a few minutes ago that no group has *the* one way, and no group judges another group in any official capacity."

Feeling agitated and threatened, I quickly jumped up. "I didn't say no OA group has *the* one way," I explained. "What I said is that we do not have the right to judge another group which does not behave in a way in which *we* perhaps might behave."

Ethel was insistent. "All right," she said. "I'm going to make a statement. I wish to know whether this Conference feels that there is one way in which to be OA, or whether they feel that there are many combinations of the formula that may work well for many different groups and many different people.

"I wish to know whether the group intends to take any stand, for instance, on whether people who are not actively practicing abstinence should be limited in their participation at any time in meetings. Is this to be left an individual thing, or is there going to be some kind of ruling on this? These are things that are important to our group.

"I wish to know whether it is the intention of OA's head office to make available fairly balanced material. . . . I wish to know if there will be some determination at Headquarters of a representative system in OA, or whether Headquarters will remain whatever you have time, energy and capacity to do. . . . Is it going to be up to one or two individuals to choose somebody to 'come in and write a piece on this,' or 'we need a mailing on that.' I want to know if there will be some legitimate channel through which the individual groups will be represented, because we will not, I don't think, participate unless there is."

By now Ethel had everyone's attention. I could see mixed emotions on the faces of the delegates in front of me as she continued speaking.

"I have been told by several people in what I call positions of authority in this organization that there will be a split right now, this weekend. I was against it being voiced, because I think the best way to get a split is to say one is coming. I'll tell you, though, that our group wishes to go along with OA, be a formal part of the OA organization, if the organization truly represents all the groups. . . . Our point of view doesn't have to carry the day, but we should have a chance . . . if we feel that it is not so rigid and and so confining that we can truly not believe it." With that, Ethel sat down, her face set in anger.

After a few seconds of dead silence, the room began to buzz. Irene remained unmoving, stone-faced. Bea and Thelma exchanged worried glances. Frankly, I was just plain scared. Was this the end? Could we reach a compromise? I uttered a silent "Help!"

The answer came at once. Slowly, A.G. unfolded his six-foot-plus frame and rose to his feet. Carefully, thoughtfully, he began to speak.

"I'd like to say something to that," he began. "I thought that this Conference had two possible objectives, two things that we very much needed to do. . . . Number one is we needed a basis for unity, and I think we found that basis for unity this morning in the Twelve Steps and Twelve Traditions. I personally feel that any group that says they're trying to work the Twelve Steps and Twelve Traditions is welcome to call themselves an OA group. . . .

"Number two, I think that after finding a basis for unity . . . then we need to lay a foundation for the future, potential growth of the OA organization. I think we might well take a little more from AA there and do what they have done. Our group is very strong for the establishment of a Board of Trustees, comparable to AA's Board of Trustees—a group of delegates from the various groups, however we would want to select them."

This was the first time anyone in OA had made such a suggestion, and A.G. had our complete and undivided attention!

"This Board of Trustees should be in a position of guiding the future progress of OA," he continued. "For AA this has worked very well. This takes the responsibility off of one person. This takes the responsibility off of any two or three persons. This, you might say, could serve to temper some of the things that we might get all fired up and try to do. I, personally . . . am capable of having some of the wildest ideas known to mankind and fervently believing them for a period of time. I need something to guide my life, and my Higher Power has helped me so far. At any rate, a Board of Trustees might do this same sort of thing for OA. It would certainly be my motion that here at this first Conference, after deciding on a basis for unity, that we elect a Board of Trustees to guide us as we go along."

Glancing at Ethel, he took a deep breath and continued on. "One more thing about your statement about how rigid it is going to be. . . . I'd like to say once more that as far as I'm concerned, any group that says they're working the Twelve Steps and Twelve Traditions to form a way in which they can eat normally, happily, is an OA group if they want to be. If they want to stand on their heads while they do this, if they want to whistle 'Dixie,' if they want to practice yoga while they do it, it suits me fine. I don't care; I'll work it my way." Finished, he abruptly sat down.

Those among us familiar with AA and its practices (which included almost every delegate) could easily recognize the principle of group autonomy behind A.G.'s colorful statement. Nobody disagreed.

By now it was nearly noon, and everyone was hungry. "Let's take our lunch break," I suggested. "Think about what's been said here, and be back at two o'clock for the afternoon session."

There was a feeling among us that OA had reached a turning point. We had a decision to make which would lay the groundwork for the kind of Fellowship which would emerge from this Conference. As we talked, we knew the survival of OA was at stake. Would we be able to agree upon a basis for unity? Could we develop a stable structure for ourselves which would bring together the warring factions?

The lunch break gave everyone a chance to talk out fears and discuss positive solutions. The majority really wanted to see OA stay together and continue to grow. The minority on both sides, still stubbornly clinging to their opinions, would be given every opportunity to discuss options for compromise. (Of course, it helped that everyone always felt better after a meal!)

When lunchtime was over, we reconvened in the meeting room. As I took my place at the leader's podium, I looked out over the fifteen delegates. Could I hope for progress? I said a silent prayer for guidance while I brought the meeting to order.

Immediately, Ethel raised her hand. Without missing a beat, she said, "We endorse as our only basic creed, the only thing that OA in general subscribes to from Headquarters is the Twelve Steps and Twelve Traditions. I make a motion that we acknowledge that these two things are the only creed that OA subscribes to, basically."

"I'll second the motion," said A.G.

At this point, the Steps and Traditions being referred to were identical to AA's, with appropriate changes from 'alcohol' and 'alcoholic' to 'food' and 'compulsive overeater.' (AA had given us permission to use them with these minor changes.)

I held my breath as I asked, "All those in favor?" Fifteen hands were raised. "All those opposed?" No one moved.

There it was: the single most important vote ever taken in OA! In this historic action—unanimous approval of the

Twelve Steps and Twelve Traditions as the basic foundation of Overeaters Anonymous—the delegates stopped talking about splitting OA apart because of our differences and began unifying us into a Fellowship because of our similarities.

Everyone applauded and smiled. We had won our first major victory, but there were many more hurdles to be jumped. Our new foundation of unity would be tested immediately.

Ethel stood up again. "The second motion," she said, "was that we create a Board of Trustees. . . . One of their duties is that they will be responsible for submitting literature for the democratic approval of the member groups, and that no literature from Headquarters is sent out until it has been submitted by the Board of Trustees and approved by the groups."

I interjected, "May I amend that to say 'by the groups' delegates at the annual Conference?'"

Ethel nodded. "Or whatever the group democratically uses. This [method of approval] would be set up by the Board of Trustees, too."

A.G. joined in here. "I have in mind a Board of Trustees that will get together in the literature that we need and develop literature along those lines. Then when this little Board of Trustees approves of it, send it out to the various groups for approval."

After a brief discussion, Ethel amended her motion. "Literature can originate at any point, but the trustees must pass on this and submit it to the OA membership for approval before it is officially available from Headquarters."

"The vote does not have to be unanimous from all the groups?" I asked.

"Oh, no," A.G. and Ethel agreed simultaneously. "By a democratic, simple majority."

This motion was unanimously approved, and a structure of service began to rise from our foundation of unity.

A sense of the importance of what was taking place now seemed to grip every person in the room. Lorraine raised her hand. "I'd like to make a motion that the proceedings of this particular convention be either mailed, one copy to each group or every single member of OA, to be sponsored by Central Service."

A.G. seconded the motion, and we unanimously voted to mail a report to each delegate.

Next, we moved forward with the construction of OA's service structure. Elated at our previous unanimous votes, I thought the rest of the day would be smooth sailing. Oh, was I wrong!

It began innocently enough when A.G. moved that "we select five persons here at the Conference to serve on the Board of Trustees, and that we elect them by passing out ballots and let each person list the five they would choose, and we take the five highest."

"Do you think five is enough?" said Ethel.

"How many do you feel?" I asked her.

"I would prefer to see seven," she urged, "because you never can get everybody together, and with five, if two don't show up, and then you've got three. . . ."

A.G. interrupted. "Well, most of this will be done by mail, anyway."

Ethel shook her head; she was furious. "I'd like to amend the motion to have seven trustees," she insisted.

Lorraine stood up. "OA will be a big group by the time next year rolls around," she said. "Even if there were only a few members here [for trustees' meetings], there may be a lot of decisions within a year."

Neither Lorraine nor Ethel was saying so, but they had both done some arithmetic and realized that their minority viewpoint, the so-called "psychological faction," had little chance of being represented on a board with only five members selected in the manner being proposed by A.G.

Ethel turned to him. "Would you accept my amendment to your motion?" she asked.

"Not yet, I haven't," A.G. replied. "I think this: the mechanics of it are going to be difficult, due to the fact that many of us live in different parts of the country. I mean, we're from Arizona, Northern California, Texas . . . a lot of different places. Golly, even you that live here in this little town of Los Angeles have trouble getting together, so I think that smaller is easier. So I would prefer to leave it at five."

Ethel persisted. "Why don't we vote on five or seven, and then vote on the resolution." A.G. agreed.

When the vote was taken, eleven delegates raised their hands in favor of a five-member board.

Carefully, A.G. restated his motion. "We elect a board of five trustees from the delegates to this Conference to handle the duties of the office of trustees until the next Conference. Their term will expire at the next Conference, and these five people are to be elected by having each person write down their five choices of names, and we'll tally them up, and the top five—the five that receive the most votes—will be the trustees."

At this point Mabel, Mildred, Bea and Thelma withdrew their names from consideration for the board, and a ballot was taken to choose OA's first five trustees from among the remaining eleven people at the Conference. When the votes were counted, Emma, A.G., Irene and I had been elected trustees. There was a tie between Sonny and Carol for the fifth position.

It was obvious that the minority faction was not represented at all, and Ethel simply refused to give up! Her voice shook with feeling as she spoke. "I have something to say."

We stopped our preparations for the tie-breaking vote, and everyone listened intently.

"I feel that in this board," she began, "one reason I wanted seven instead of five was that I know that my group's point of view is democratically very much outnumbered. I had hoped that one of us would be on the board, and I consider it a very sad thing for us that I must go back to my group and say that . . . these people who stress the spiritual at the expense . . . of the rest [now appear to represent all of OA]. . . . We will not be very happy about participating wholeheartedly if we don't feel that our point of view is understood and expressed. Not that we wish to dominate, but we don't wish to be so dominated and so outnumbered that we don't have any normal avenue of expression. . . . I feel it is against all of Robert's Rules and maybe even good sportsmanship, but I don't think good sportsmanship should have a place when you represent a group. I must tell you that I feel we have no real representation on the Board of Trustees, and I believe that this is the beginning of a schism that was spoken about if we leave it this way."

Having issued her ultimatum, Ethel sat down defiantly. The room was dead quiet; no one moved.

Ever the mediator, A.G. asked Ethel, "How would you select the trustees?"

After a moment she answered, "Well, I should have spoken sooner, A.G., and I made a halfhearted attempt by asking that it be seven. I should have said then that I feared that this would not give us a chance, since we are apparently a minority. You either can say that a minority should have no voice, or you can say that since you're a minority, some special dispensation, some acknowledgement should be taken."

Poor A.G. He'd come from Texas with such high hopes for meeting with other Twelve-Stepping compulsive overeaters. Instead, he found himself in the middle of a major fight. He was having a hard time understanding Ethel's viewpoint and why she felt she was a minority not represented on the board.

Now he said, "I get the very distinct feeling, Ethel, that you want something here that we are not doing, that you want us to express something or to approve something, and I really don't know what it is."

After describing how her meeting functioned, Ethel explained, "My basic philosophy, speaking for my group, is, as I've said many times today, that this [OA] is a three-pronged attack: the spiritual, the emotional and the physical. We do not believe that the *only* approach is God as you see Him."

"You think the Twelve Steps is just Step Three?" asked A.G.

"No, we don't," she replied. "We admit there is a Power greater than ourselves, but we do not name Him. And we do not say this is the supreme portion of the way. We say it is three inseparable assets. We got emotionally sick . . . and we can be helped spiritually, emotionally and of course, physically. . . . What OA means to us is these three things. What AA means is these three things."

Now it was clear! Ethel had finally defined her group's point of view and talked about OA as a three-part program. She was right, of course, but many delegates were so worked up from the arguments of the past year that they either didn't hear her or didn't completely understand what she was trying to achieve. They still didn't realize that she and her group had moved beyond an emphasis on psychology towards the three elements of the OA and AA programs—spiritual, emotional and physical.

Puzzled, A.G. said, "What do you think we are going to do as a Board of Trustees that would be inconsistent with this?"

"You're not going to do anything bad," Ethel answered. "It's just that you're not going to handle the other aspects adequately for me."

A delegate asked her a question, to which she replied, "No, I do not want literature on psychiatry . . . let's have that [be] clear. . . . We are not a psychiatric group. We are trying to practice OA on a three-pronged program."

At this point, I suggested that we go around the room so that everyone would have a chance to talk.

Lorraine added her voice to Ethel's, saying that the Tuesday night, Thursday night and Monday afternoon groups ought to have representation on the board for their point of view and method of working the program.

She then went on to describe her meeting's format in detail. "This is a wonderful, strong group," she continued. "It is the mother group . . . started on Tuesday. Other people have found their way, and we have found our way. . . . I, personally, believe that the Tuesday group will become non-existent if I go home and report to them we have no representation for our way of observing."

"Not non-existent," Ethel interrupted, "but not existent as OA. . . ."

"Oh, they've definitely agreed already that OA is just a title," Lorraine said. "They would love very much to be a part of that title, but they don't have to be a part of that title. It would make a great deal of sense to have unity; that's what OA means. . . ."

Sonny spoke next. She described her small Valley group and its meeting format in great detail. "We are a very practical group. There's no one that denies the spiritual, but most of them think that this is not the only way. . . . The basic philosophy of our group is flexibility. . . ."

A.G. sighed, his brow furrowed. "In substance," he said at last, "we have been handed a take-it-or-leave-it. They feel that they are entitled to representation on the Board of Trustees. In the vote that was taken, they did not receive this representation. They feel their groups would disassociate if they do not receive this representation."

He paused, looking around the room. "I wonder this," he continued. "I'm certainly not working it like they are, not by a long shot, but unity does mean a whole lot. If they're trying to work the Twelve Steps and Twelve Traditions, would we be wrong to stretch our tolerance to say 'let's add one member onto the Board of Trustees and select one of these two to be on it?'" He indicated Ethel and Lorraine.

Although Bea was from one of the Valley groups, she agreed, saying, "Lorraine, Ethel and Sonny represent enough people to have a voice. . . . OA unity as a whole is the thing that is important."

Even if they disagreed on other matters, at the mention of unity most of the delegates nodded their heads.

"Well then," said A.G., "I move to elect either Ethel or Lorraine to the Board of Trustees."

There was a flurry of hand-raising and general cross-talk. After more discussion, A.G. stood up. "I'd like to make a motion to amend the previous motion to put seven members on the Board of Trustees, and that the two who were tied, Carol and Sonny, both be accepted, . . . and that Ethel's name be added to the Board of Trustees." The motion passed easily, and I heaved a sigh of relief.

In looking back, it's clear that A.G.'s appearance in our little Fellowship had probably saved the day. He was a Texan from Gluttons Anonymous and therefore had been totally removed from all our arguments. In addition, he was a man, and OA had been comprised only of women. The blending of genders gave OA a much-needed balance. Finally, A.G.'s professional expertise filled a void in our operations and helped us establish stability in OA's business affairs.

Thirty-three years later, A.G. would describe the events of that day to the visitors at the 1995 World Service Convention in Minneapolis, Minnesota. "You have to recognize," he said, "we were all scared to death this thing was going to fall apart, and we'd go back where we'd been. We were all terrified. We were all afraid that if we made the slightest wrong move, it'd all go 'pouf,' and it'd be lost, and we'd be back fat again. So it was a sensitive, sensitive thing that we were trying to handle with great care, and we were very touchy about it. So that engendered a lot of conflict, but by the grace of God we survived and the organization survived."

After the trustees' election had been settled, we turned our attention to the setup of our little General Service Office. I described the work I'd been doing since our first meeting. I'd brought some of the office files to show the delegates. I'd also brought letters received since the Paul Coates telecast, along with our reply letters. Next, I outlined how I'd set up the files and established proper office procedure. I finished with, "This job takes at least four to five hours a day."

After a long discussion on the office and the need for a secretary and a treasurer, Lorraine said, "I move that Rozanne be given the official title of national secretary."

"I second the motion," said A.G., "and I think we ought to commend her at the same time for having done a tremendous job."

I smiled and accepted. After all the disagreements, it was wonderful to feel appreciated.

The delegates then discussed the need for a treasurer. Maureen from the Castro Valley group in Northern California suggested we find somebody with a working knowledge of bookkeeping. The trustees would be given the task of finding someone.

Meanwhile, I remembered that when I first suggested this Conference, I had envisioned a meeting of delegates every year—an annual OA Business Conference. May was an ideal time to get together. The weather was beautiful in Los Angeles, and summer vacation time had not yet started.

Therefore, I said, "I make a motion that the next Conference and each Conference thereafter be held annually in the middle of May." The motion was seconded, and the vote was unanimous. A May Conference of OA delegates, first from all over the United States and later from all over the world, has been held every year since that day in 1962.

Encouraged by our positive, productive discussion after all the heated uproar, I then brought up the financial support of our General Service Office. I explained the current costs, and we discussed what the groups were doing to contribute. Our most pressing need was to have a reserve on hand to pay for printing, without waiting to accumulate enough money from literature sales.

Several groups were already contributing half of their Seventh-Tradition money every month. Others were contributing less but were waiting for the Conference decision. Ethel suggested that we aim for the ability to send literature at no cost to help new groups get started. It was agreed that each group would try to contribute in the manner which suited its individual needs.

We then talked about the forty-page booklet I'd adapted from AA's "Big Book." I told them AA had denied us reprint permission, and everyone agreed it was a shame we couldn't publish the booklet.

Thelma was enthusiastic, saying, "I'm all for the ideas; I wouldn't change one of them. But I think we can get by with the materials we have at the present time."

After some discussion, the general consensus was that the booklet should be rewritten and presented to the groups before the next Conference in May, 1963.

(In fact, it would be seventeen years before OA would publish a book of its own about our program, and twenty-seven years before we would publish a book about the Twelve Steps. During all those years we would use AA's "Big Book" and "Twelve and Twelve" in our meetings, changing the wording to apply to us.)

Then there was the matter of the name of our Fellowship. Although it was not recorded in those first Conference minutes, A.G. says, "I remember a discussion, and probably a vote, on the name of the organization. I know we Texans were all disappointed that Gluttons Anonymous wasn't accepted, and there was considerable discussion about it with the groups when we returned [to Texas] with our report."

However, there were sixteen OA groups and five Gluttons Anonymous groups. Overeaters Anonymous was the choice of the majority. (The minutes of the 1963 Conference, described in Chapter Nine, would show that we reaffirmed this name with another majority vote.)

It was getting late in the afternoon, but we were determined to follow our agenda. Introducing the next topic, I said, "Our last item concerns national publicity for OA. Let me tell you about the response from the Paul Coates show." Then I went on to talk about the five hundred letters we'd received and how much work it had been for our fledgling group just to answer the mail. "And yet," I smiled at them, "almost everybody sitting here today came in due to that television interview."

The members looked at each other, nodding and laughing. "Do we want to use Paul Coates again?" I asked them, "or should we continue to strengthen ourselves and use the Board of Trustees to help the groups gain strength and unity with one another?"

As the delegates discussed publicity, most felt their groups weren't yet strong enough to handle the influx of newcomers that might result from national publicity. Many of the groups had already done some publicity on the local level. Most listed their meetings in community calendar listings. A.G. even told of an advertisement the Gluttons Anonymous groups in Texas had run which read, "If you are greatly overweight and want to stay that way, that's your business. If you have tried to reduce and cannot, that's our business."

Lorraine spoke out for the still-suffering compulsive overeater. She described the West Los Angeles group's experience of having a large influx of new members when an article appeared in the local *Santa Monica Outlook* newspaper. "The need is much too great for us to be selfish," she said. "We'll have volunteers within OA to handle the Twelfth-Step work that results from publicity. I'm in favor of doing the Paul Coates show again, maybe a second anniversary sort of thing."

After much discussion, Ethel moved that until the following year, we limit our publicity efforts to the Paul Coates show, if it is offered, and to whatever local publicity the groups wanted to do. Lorraine restated the motion in a more positive manner. "I move," she said, "we do appear on the Paul Coates show for the purposes of furthering our Twelfth-Step work and helping people who need this program." The motion passed easily.

By now we were all tired, but exhilarated. It was after 5:30, and we had successfully completed the agenda for the meeting. We had a short planning session for the following day, and then at 5:45, OA's first Fellowship-wide business meeting was adjourned.

"We did it!" I said to myself, feeling triumphant. It had been a long and difficult day, but together we had laid the foundation for what would someday become the worldwide Fellowship of Overeaters Anonymous.

Chapter Seven

Our Trusted Trustees

HE next day dawned full of hope and the prospect of hard work. Sunday's meetings would be momentous. In the morning the Board of Trustees was to hold its first meeting, and in the afternoon we were going to have an open meeting where delegates would share their experience, strength and hope. This open session was to be the forerunner of OA's annual Convention, a gathering which would eventually encompass OA members from around the world.

Sunday morning, August 12, 1962, at eleven o'clock, the seven of us who had been elected to the first Board of Trustees gathered in the conference room.

In addition to A.G. and me, that first Board of Trustees included Emma W. from Arizona, Sonny B., Carol G., Irene B. and Ethel K. As we settled ourselves, I looked around at the players in the drama which was about to unfold.

Emma had started a different Overeaters Anonymous near Phoenix, Arizona, about the same time we were starting OA in Southern California. Neither of us knew the other existed until April, 1961, after the Paul Coates interview, when Emma's sister came to our Tuesday night meeting and gave me the Arizona address. Emma was a tall, slender woman with a softspoken, gentle manner. Older than some of us, Emma had solid AA experience and had modeled her groups on the Twelve Steps. They were delighted to merge with us, and Emma came to our Conference representing groups in Tempe, Mesa and Phoenix.

Sonny was a bright, vivacious young woman who had joined OA shortly after the Paul Coates telecast. Not quite yet at her normal weight, she had enthusiastically embraced the OA program. Sonny's Valley group was an offshoot of a Los Angeles group; thus it wasn't part of the "spiritual-only" contingent.

Carol was a tall, very sweet young woman with a magnificent complexion. She had lost considerable weight and had more to go. Her father had been in AA for many years, so she had grown up with Twelve-Step principles. An active church-goer, she was very spiritual, but she wasn't part of any OA faction.

I thought of Irene and Ethel as the principle combatants in the "spiritual-psychological" battle, primarily because they were both very strong, outspoken women.

Prior to the Conference, Ethel had advocated a psychological approach to the Twelve Steps. She had been a domineering influence ever since she came to OA, and she continued her influence during the business meeting. At that time she had lost some weight and still had more to lose. Ethel was brilliant and analytical, and she had a good intellectual grasp of the Twelve-Step program. Above all, she was determined to prevent the spiritual advocates from making the OA message too religious.

Irene was the leader of the spiritual faction. She was a tall, slender, charismatic redhead who firmly believed she had the only answer for all compulsive overeaters. Very independent, she kept the rest of us continually off balance, wondering what she was going to do next with "her" OA groups. A.G. would remark later that Irene was a person who always had to have a cause. This weekend her cause was making sure OA meetings and literature strongly emphasized the spiritual basis of the program. Once a compromise was reached between Irene's and Ethel's views, Irene developed another cause, one which was to affect OA for many years. (But that's another chapter!)

On this Sunday morning, as we joined hands to say the Serenity Prayer, we all felt that this meeting was an important occasion for OA.

Our first act was to elect a chairman, and A.G. was our unanimous choice. For an organization that had banned men only the year before, this election was certainly a change of events! Yet it seemed a natural choice at the time. Years later A.G. would say he was elected because he was a neutral outsider. My own feeling was that he was a man with the business expertise and experience the rest of us sorely lacked. Whatever the reason, he provided practicality and leadership at a crucial point in OA's development.

That morning we decided that there would be no quorum meetings of the board. All seven members had to be present, or all would vote by mail. "And our next task," said A.G., "is to elect a secretary for this board. I'd like to nominate Rozanne." The vote was unanimous. My new position blended well with the one I'd been given the day before as national secretary of OA's General Service Office.

At this point in OA's growth, there was barely enough money to cover the expenses of running our little office (which was still rent-free in my dining room), printing directories and *OA Bulletins*, renting the post office box and installing our new telephone. Thus, there was no money left to pay me a salary. I considered my OA work a labor of love.

However, I did have another labor of love which came first—my family. Debbie and Julie were still very little, neither one in kindergarten yet. I had a home to run and my wonderful, ever-patient Marvin to care for. I just couldn't continue to do all of the work; there weren't enough hours in the day.

Therefore, as we considered the office setup, we agreed OA would need a treasurer with bookkeeping background. JoAnne P. from one of the Valley groups was nominated and unanimously elected.

We decided that each delegate would report on the Conference to his or her area committee or group.

113

We also talked about how closely we should follow AA. The general consensus was that we would not have an AA member advising us in any official capacity on how to set up and run OA. We said, "Any help that we receive unofficially and informally from our AA friends is most welcome, of course."

Our next topic was to fundamentally affect OA's business affairs for many decades. A.G. began the discussion. "It's obvious," he said, "that OA has need of structure at the national level. OA cannot continue to spread the word—and that has to be our primary purpose as covered in the Traditions— without some sort of structure to control its ability to promote itself. Attraction rather than promotion is great, but somehow or other there has to be publicity, and there needs to be a source of accepted and approved data about any national organization before the news media are going to touch it.

"What OA needs is a way to raise some money from its members, to provide literature for those members and for the news media and for newcomers who might come along. In order to do those things, we need a Board of Trustees [which was elected yesterday]. We need bylaws so that we all understand what we are doing and how we are going to do it, and we need a 501(C)(3) classification from the Internal Revenue Service."

"And what is that?" I asked.

"That's for non-taxable, charitable organizations," he answered.

Since most of us didn't have A.G.'s experience in these matters, we listened intently to what he was saying. No one objected to his suggestions; everyone agreed that these were things we needed to do. "Let's also read AA's Third Legacy Manual," someone suggested. All heads nodded.

Years later, A.G. was to remember, "The original Bylaws, (Guidelines we called them then) were written by an attorney in Austin, Texas, free of charge. His name was Sander W. Shapiro. [Although not a compulsive overeater], his contribution to OA was made on the basis that he saw what it had done for me in my life and wanted to be a part of that. Sandy even attended a couple of our early trustees' meetings to help explain the technical side of the business arrangements."

During that first board meeting, we also approved A.G.'s idea of incorporating Overeaters Anonymous as a non-profit organization. The final version of the Guidelines and incorporation papers was done by another [non-OA-member] Texas attorney, Denver E. Perkins, for the modest fee of $150. Of course, the result of all this was that OA was first incorporated as an association in the state of Texas.

(In 1968 Bruce Gleason, a California attorney, began the process of establishing OA as a California corporation. On December 15, 1968, our Articles of Incorporation were officially approved, which made us a California non-profit corporation. On May 16, 1969, we received our federal tax-exempt status. At the 1969 National Conference, Bruce ended his presentation with the quip, "All I can say is that I wish my own personal health was as healthy as the legal health of this corporation.")

Meanwhile, back at the first trustees' meeting in August, 1962, it suddenly became apparent that the new trustees had a lot of work to do, and the hour we'd allotted to get the board organized was quickly drawing to a close.

A.G. appointed us all to committees: Irene and I were to discuss and recommend operating rules for the board meetings. Ethel and Sonny were to draw up regulations as to how our finances should be handled. Emma and Carol would come up with a set of rules for the elections of delegates to the annual Conference. These committees were to meet and submit written reports to me by September 25, so that I could distribute them to the trustees a month ahead of the October 25 board meeting.

It was close to noon, and we were all hungry. Agreeing that it was time for lunch and that we would have to meet again that night after the open sharing session, we adjourned.

In retrospect, I believe that we were all so busy we did not feel the full impact of what had just occurred—OA had just had its first effective trustees' meeting! Although there would be hundreds more in the years ahead, this meeting was special, because it showed us we could function efficiently as a business organization. This would be vital if OA's groups were to unite and grow into a worldwide Fellowship.

After supper on Sunday night, our new Board of Trustees met again, along with JoAnne P., who had agreed to serve as OA's first treasurer. With the afternoon sharing session, it had been a full day, but now we really got down to business.

A motion was made and seconded that "Rozanne be allowed to pay current expenses and current bills and maintain the office in accordance with what she has done in the past until we do get our Bylaws completely set up and our financial committee comes in with a set of rules to control these things." The vote in favor was unanimous.

Next on the agenda was printing. The question was raised, "How many of each Conference-approved pamphlet should be printed?" After a short discussion, Irene, Lorraine and I were appointed as a "printing committee" to secure the best possible price quotes on one thousand of each pamphlet.

A.G. reminded us that some pieces needed rewriting. "These," he said, "must be sent to the board for approval [of the new copy] before printing." We decided to tentatively set the prices at cost-and-a-half of printing to cover all the expenses, including mailing.

In addition, we agreed to have one thousand sheets of stationery and one thousand envelopes printed with only the General Service Office post office box address.

Ethel volunteered to look into the matter of how to set up OA legally to avoid tax problems. Her report was to be due October 1, 1962.

Next, a motion was made, seconded and unanimously approved that ten Conference *Bulletins* would be sent to each group, to be distributed as the delegates saw fit. Further *Bulletins* would be approved and sent when the board felt it was necessary.

A motion was made, seconded and unanimously approved that "included in our first *Bulletin* should be one or two stories taken from the tape of the Sunday afternoon Conference. These stories shall be left to the discretion of the committee taking care of the *Bulletin*, and they will edit them. Permission must be gotten from each individual . . . before printing."

Moving on, we came to a subject dear to my heart. I remembered how I had desperately tried to find TOPS after my first visit to Gamblers Anonymous. At the time, I couldn't locate any group because they weren't listed in the Los Angeles telephone directory.

As a result, I'd always strongly advocated a listing for OA, and that night the board agreed with me. They authorized me to list an OA phone number in the Los Angeles telephone directory, using GSO funds. They also said that "an answering service isn't a good idea, because when a person calls, a recovered overeater should be there to answer." In addition, I was instructed to mimeograph new group meeting directories. Under the column, "For information, call . . . " I was to put the delegates' names.

Although we had all agreed that we were not ready for national publicity, permission was given to the Arizona groups to put a Conference notice in the *Arizona Republic*.

Objections were raised to the pictures which were taken during the Sunday sharing session, and the trustees voted that "picture-taking is absolutely forbidden during any Conference or OA meeting." They also said that all board meetings would be open to any OA or AA members who wanted to attend.

By this time I was beginning to feel overwhelmed by all the work ahead of me. There would be board secretarial work, committee meetings, GSO correspondence and other office duties all to be added to the heavy load I was already carrying.

I told the board there just weren't enough hours in the day for me to accomplish everything. Ethel volunteered to help answer some of the letters. That was a relief, and I agreed, as long as she returned them to me for approval before mailing.

As the meeting approached the end, the trustees offered a vote of thanks to JoAnne and A.G.

Before we closed, A.G. stood up. In his first official statement to the board as its chairman, he graciously acknowledged this moment in OA's history when the Fellowship stopped being mine to control and became the responsibility of its elected trusted servants:

"If anybody deserves any credit here, it's Rozanne," he said. "She's done something that I doubt I would have been big enough to do. I wonder if all of us realize what Rozanne has really done here during this Conference. She was the original OA; she has been the founder all the way through. It took many years before Bill W. was willing or able to consider turning AA over to a Board of Trustees. This she has done with no tears, with no quibbling, with no hollering, with no nothing, and I think she is to be very much commended for it." I had tears in my eyes as my fellow trustees applauded his words.

Many years later, Beverly R., a long-time member, told me, "Rozanne, I believe that first Conference, held so soon after starting OA, contributed more than any other factor to the early growth of OA."

In reflecting on Beverly's statement, I had to agree. We had begun the Conference deeply divided, with each faction threatening withdrawal from OA. We ended it united in a common solution to our desperate problem of compulsive overeating, and we laid the groundwork for a unified Fellowship in the years to come.

Chapter Eight

Conventional Wisdom

URING the June planning sessions for our first Conference, it occurred to several of us that we ought to have something besides a day-long business meeting.

"Let's make it an open OA meeting," someone suggested. "How about a time for sharing, where we each tell our story?"

That idea brought an enthusiastic response from everyone. We decided that Sunday afternoon would be perfect. We would have had all day Saturday to discuss business; the next afternoon we would have a few hours to tell what we were like, what happened and what we were like now.

All OA members would be invited. Then one of the members suggested, "Let's ask our friends and families to come, too, as well as our AA supporters. It's a great time to let them hear what we've been doing since we came to OA."

Thus the annual OA Convention was born. From 1962 through 1977, the Conventions would be held immediately following the end of the yearly Business Conference in Los Angeles.

All day Saturday, August 11, 1962, the delegates had worked diligently to establish a firm foundation for their beloved organization. Sunday morning the trustees had met, continuing with the business affairs of OA.

Now Sunday afternoon had arrived, and it was time for fellowship and fun! The room filled rapidly; everyone was relaxed and looking forward to this new experience in OA.

119

Irene opened the meeting. She smiled as she came to the podium, waiting for the chattering to quiet down. "It is a privilege," she began, "to be the leader of your first delegates' report from your Convention. What you're going to hear today is a demonstration of how we run an open meeting in the Valley. . . . We always open our meetings with the Serenity Prayer. . . . Listen to this prayer with your heart because this embodies everything we believe that this OA program means to us."

After we all joined in saying the Serenity Prayer, Irene read from portions of the first page of our original four-page booklet. She also introduced our newly-revised Twelve Traditions.

Next, Emma read the opening portion of "How It Works" from Chapter Five of the AA "Big Book." A.G. then presented our newly-adopted Twelve Steps.

"The next part of our reading," Irene went on, "is the Twelve Unifying Rules. This will tell the newcomer and the visitors more about our program than anything we've said yet. . . . This is a loosely-knit Fellowship, the most loosely-knit organization in the world. . . . People come to this because they want it." She then asked Norma from Texas to read the Rules. (The Traditions had been adopted only the day before and had not yet been incorporated into meeting formats.)

When Norma finished, Irene introduced all the delegates who'd been at our first Business Conference. They all stood to receive enthusiastic applause. Everyone was smiling; we could feel the joy in the room!

"Now comes the time," Irene continued, "to introduce you to one of our founders. Our founder is very important to me. I'll only tell you this . . . that I feel personally that every Fellowship, every business, every organization in the world is really the extended shadow of one person. May I introduce that person [OA's founder] to you now—Rozanne."

Walking up to the podium, I felt a surge of gratitude for Irene's heartfelt introduction.

"Thank you, Irene," I smiled at her. "At least it's a longer, narrower shadow than it used to be." The audience laughed, and I felt a little less frightened.

"I'm Rozanne, a compulsive overeater," I began. "I'm very happy to see all these faces. This is a time of great significance for Overeaters Anonymous as a Fellowship and for all of the suffering compulsive overeaters everywhere who are alone, afraid, misunderstood and crying out for help.

"As many of you know, we have just completed our first National Conference, composed of the delegates from most OA groups now existing across the country. We are continuing to practice those principles of unity which will ensure recovery for all of us as individuals and as groups. We stand united now under these Twelve Steps and Twelve Traditions which you heard read today, united in a common solution to a problem which threatens to wreck our lives and destroy our thinking—the progressive illness we call compulsive overeating.

"Some of you may think that this organization is quite unique, that our practice is quite unique, and this isn't entirely so. Our principles of personal recovery are borrowed, and most of our structural ideas have been borrowed and adapted to our own needs. We are another link in a long chain by which men and women for hundreds of years have tried to bind themselves together to relieve their common problem.

"Overeaters Anonymous is a remarkable Fellowship. It embraces love, acceptance without judgement and, above all, self-sacrifice on the part of the individual and the group. Our recovery is assured only so long as we remember to practice our principles in all our affairs, and to carry this precious message to the compulsive overeater who still suffers.

"In the future, I'm sure that Overeaters Anonymous, individually and as a Fellowship, will make mistakes. We need not fear these mistakes as long as we remember to confess them, to admit them and to correct them at once. False pride, anger and resentment are three characteristic defects we possess which we must be ever-vigilant against for their reappearance.

"OA isn't a new religion. We must remember, always,

with humility, that its principles have been borrowed from centuries-old ideas. The Fellowships which have gone before us have also borrowed these principles. This has gone back hundreds upon hundreds of years.

"It would also be a result of our false pride to believe that we alone are a cure-all for compulsive overeating. [As Bill W. said,] 'We owe a debt to the men in medicine, a debt to the men in psychiatry, and a debt to the spiritual leaders of those who believe this way.'

"Together there are many ways for the overeater to cure a desperate problem. We in OA have found one solution, and it has been remarkable. We have believed that alone we have no willpower to correct this condition, that with the help of a Power greater than ourselves, be it the concept of another person, the group, or a spiritual power of our own individual understanding, we have taken these Twelve Steps and set them for ourselves on the long road for recovery.

"We have a long way to go in OA. We have many wonderful precepts of other Fellowships to look back on to help us and to guide us. As I said, I'm sure we'll make our own mistakes, but I think we have started on the right road.

"If we, as groups and individuals, keep in mind always that there are hundreds of thousands of people around us who are drowning in a well of despair and fright and don't know where to turn, if we can reach out our hands to help these people, if we can share what we have learned, if we can apply it to all areas of our lives, we will have indeed performed the task for which we have been placed on this earth.

"There are others waiting to hear the answer. There are many of us here who have applied this program, each in his own or her own individual way, and you'll hear them today. Many interpretations, but one common solution. For us, and for all those who are still suffering, may God help us—and them—as we try to help ourselves together."

When I finished speaking, Irene brought the delegates to the podium, one at a time, to share their experience, strength and hope. Thirteen of the fifteen delegates spoke that day, telling their own stories of how OA had affected their lives.

When they finished talking, Irene said, "This is our last report, and Rozanne has a closing she would like to share with us."

"By the way," I began, "someone asked me during the break . . . I came into OA at 161 and today I weigh 103, a weight loss of 58 pounds.

"This is a brief closing for this meeting. You've heard the delegates from our first Conference. We hope that we have reached at least one person in this audience who may be in need of help. Or perhaps through the people here, we will have reached one person, because this is just one day, and that's all we can ask for.

"We want to thank all of you for your attention and for your interest. . . . We hope that OA will progress and will grow, that each year there will be this sort of Conference and that those of you who have helped us and supported us from the beginning will continue to be here, because our gratitude to you goes beyond more than any words can say. I just, again, want to thank you and turn this over to Irene. It has been a very welcome afternoon for all of us. God bless you all."

Then Irene made some announcements, after which we passed the Seventh-Tradition basket. Finally, we closed with the Lord's Prayer.

We were all feeling relaxed. OA's business foundation had been established and many compromises had been reached. I remember feeling the glow of achievement and thinking that sunny days were ahead for us.

Chapter Nine

The OA
Guidelines

hectic, exciting nine months followed our first National Conference in August, 1962. Soon it was May, 1963, and we were about to convene for the second time. Several items were to be discussed which would affect OA for years to come, including the new OA Guidelines (the forerunner of our Bylaws).

OA had grown rapidly; this second Conference was more than twice as large as the first. Last year we'd had twenty-one groups; this year we would welcome delegates representing forty-eight groups. Two women were coming from Austin, Texas. The others were representing groups from Southern and Northern California.

We also had our seven-person Board of Trustees, elected during the first Conference, including Emma from Arizona and our lone Texas male, A.G.

On May 11, 1963, we all gathered at Sportsman's Lodge in the San Fernando Valley. First-time delegates were warmly greeted; delegates from last year happily renewed friendships.

A.G., as chairman of the board, brought the meeting to order. "Good morning, everybody," he drawled. "I'm A.G., a glutton and a compulsive overeater." "Hi, A.G.," we all responded enthusiastically. The Conference was on its way!

Glancing at his notes, he began his opening remarks by describing the new OA Conference Guidelines. "These Guidelines are to let us have a [national] basis to operate on," he said. "We have drawn up the Guidelines, which are rules of order . . . to let us know where we are. As you notice at the top of the page it says 'The Guidelines of the National Conference of Overeaters Anonymous.' Now, these Guidelines do not apply in any way to any group. The groups are each autonomous. These Guidelines apply only to the meeting here today, the National Conference of Overeaters Anonymous.

"Beyond this Conference, what do we need? We need some sort of a legal entity . . . for two things. One is that as we sell literature, as we take in and handle funds, certainly the profits that are made on the literature are to be reinvested in literature. If we just leave it as it is now, we are going to be liable for federal income tax on any profits that are made, and we'll have only fifty percent of the profits left to reinvest in literature. Our aim here is certainly not personal profit; . . . it is charitable. Consequently, we feel that this should be set up as a charitable foundation. So what we have done here . . . is to set a basis for an OA Foundation whose directors are the trustees of Overeaters Anonymous. This will let us have a charitable foundation tax-exempt status. And any contributions made from one person directly to the OA Foundation will be tax deductible. Are there any questions about that?"

The room was silent; the delegates shook their heads. A.G. grinned and heaved a sigh of relief.

Setting aside our tax-exempt status for the moment, we began our major discussion of the day: The Guidelines of the National Conference (forerunner of our Bylaws). Our Articles of Incorporation and Guidelines had been drawn up by Texas attorney, Denver E. Perkins.

Article One read: "The name of this organization shall be The National Conference of Overeaters Anonymous." Irene jumped up. "I make a motion that we keep the name Overeaters Anonymous as the name of the national Fellowship," she exclaimed. When the vote was taken, thirty-six delegates had voted "yes." Our name was to remain, and Article One was accepted.

The Texas delegates were still unhappy. The year before

they had wanted the name of their original five groups, Gluttons Anonymous, to be the name of this growing Fellowship. Even though they had been overruled at the first Conference by OA's sixteen-group majority, hope springs eternal.

When the vote was taken at this second Conference, they regretfully, but gracefully, accepted the will of the majority.

Article Two had only a minor change. Article Three contained the Twelve Steps, identical to those of AA with appropriate changes for our own compulsion. The Steps were accepted unanimously.

Next we came to the first major change of the afternoon. Article Four listed the Twelve Traditions. Tradition Three stated, "The only requirement for OA membership is a desire to stop overeating."

Our original Twelve Unifying Rules had stated: "The only requirement for OA membership is an honest desire to stop overeating and to effect a change in eating habits."

I remember the night I was rewriting those Rules to read more like AA's Twelve Traditions, so that we could include them in our literature. Sitting at the typewriter, I wrote, ". . . a desire to stop overeating." "No, no," I said to myself, "that's not good enough. It should be 'stop overeating *compulsively.*'" I sighed. "That's not right either." Because I was still a perfectionist, I insisted to myself, "It isn't enough to stop *overeating* compulsively. We must stop *eating* compulsively. That's closer to the concept of abstinence." I wrote it both ways again and stared at the two versions for several minutes. Then I said to myself, "If we're going to do this, it has to include everything."

With that I typed, "The only requirement for OA membership is a desire to stop eating compulsively." We put that statement in the literature we printed during the next year.

Therefore, when we came to the Conference examination of Tradition Three, I stood up to explain how the Tradition was being printed in our pamphlets.

After considerable discussion, the motion was made and seconded that the Guidelines be amended to be the same as the literature. The vote was forty-six to two, and Tradition Three was changed to read, "The only requirement for OA membership is a desire to stop eating compulsively."

(I didn't realize it at the time, but in voting to word our Tradition this way, we were opening the doors of Overeaters Anonymous to anyone with an eating disorder of any kind, not just overeaters.) The wording of that requirement was to come up again in future Conferences, but the delegates' vote has always been to retain the wording we approved in 1963.

Articles Five through Seven were accepted as proposed or with minor changes. Article Eight seemed to be sailing through the same way, until we came to Section 8.17.

There were very strong feelings among the delegates that the trustees should represent physical recovery in Overeaters Anonymous. Many members believed that the board was the highest level of OA service. They felt that the trustees might be called upon to talk to professionals in the medical field and in the public media. These delegates firmly believed that overweight representatives would send a negative message about the effectiveness of the OA recovery program.

Thus, the final wording in that section read:

> To be eligible to be a trustee, a person must be a member of a local group of O.A. and one who has arrested his illness of compulsive overeating. Those elected at the regular annual meeting in 1964 must then be at their normal weight. Those elected at the regular annual meeting in 1965 must have maintained their normal weight for six months prior thereto. Those elected at the regular annual meeting in 1966 and thereafter must, at the time of their election, have maintained their normal weight for one year prior thereto in O.A. Each person shall be the sole judge of what is his normal weight.

Next we took up Section 8.18. There was much concern at that 1963 Conference about the need for physical recovery on the board. What happens, many delegates asked, if a trustee is elected and starts to gain weight? The general feeling was that a return to overeating clouds the thinking, minimizing effective service. How should such a case be handled?

After a long discussion, the motion was made, seconded and passed that the wording in Section 8.18 be changed to read:

> Any trustee who advises the Board of Trustees that he has returned to compulsive overeating will be considered as having resigned as of the moment of receipt of such notice by the Board of Trustees. . . .

For many years the OA trustees took this last Section very seriously. Just before the 1963 Conference, Sonny B. became the first trustee to resign because she had slipped. In her letter of resignation to A.G., she wrote, "I have not only failed to maintain [abstinence], but have failed to lose weight. For these reasons, I feel it is not right for me to sit on a board of the one thing I value most next to my family."

In September of 1963, I also resigned as trustee under the provisions of Section 8.18. At the time I had been overeating and had begun to gain weight.

Even A.G. was not immune. Although his weight gain was not yet noticeable, on December 14, 1964, he sent a letter to the trustees which read in part:

> In accordance with Section 8.18 of the OA Guidelines, this is my notice to the Board of Trustees that I have slipped and that my resignation is effective immediately, both as Chairman of the Board and as a Trustee. I don't expect that anyone is surprised that I have slipped, but even I am surprised that I ever, by the Grace of God, found that courage and the humility to admit it. I have rationalized this thing for quite a while now—how long I really don't know and don't care. . . . If there were any way that I could be honest with myself and work the program without sending you this resignation, I would certainly do so. . . . Admitting this slip, first at the meeting last night and this morning via this letter to you, is good for me. Today I don't have to live a lie—maybe I can get honest with myself.

A.G. struggled in OA for four more unhappy years. He left in 1968, regaining 100 pounds. Then, after eighteen years, his expected miracle became a reality. He returned to Overeaters Anonymous on January 9, 1986, and began to abstain from compulsive overeating. He lost 100 pounds and has been maintaining his normal weight for many years. In a letter to me on August 19, 1995, he explained:

> It [my 1964 resignation] might serve as a suggestion to future generations that Trustees who are eating compulsively and not at normal size should get out of the way and not try to give away something they don't have!

During OA's early years, we all felt the significance of those sentiments. (I resigned as national secretary on May 21, 1965, because I had returned to compulsive overeating.) Over the next few years, several trustees resigned from the board long before their weight gain was apparent. It was important to all OA members that our trustees represent to themselves, to other OA members and to the world in general that the principles embodied in the Twelve Steps really did help us stop overeating so that we could attain and maintain a normal body size.

Now, at our second Conference, having settled that very important issue, the delegates moved on to consider the rest of the Guidelines. The discussion on the remaining articles was brief, and everything else was accepted.

Next on the agenda was the reading of the Articles of Incorporation. Following this presentation, the amended Guidelines and Articles of Incorporation were accepted by unanimous vote. (It would be 1974 before the title of the Guidelines would be changed to "Bylaws of the World Service Conference of Overeaters Anonymous.")

As the Conference ended on this bright May afternoon in 1963, we felt OA's business foundation had been established, a solid basis for our beloved Fellowship in the years ahead. Despite our differences of opinion in some areas, we all agreed that our promise of recovery from compulsive overeating lay in those magnificent Twelve Steps and Twelve Traditions. With this unanimity, we had begun to create a haven of hope for ourselves.

The Show Must Go On!

Y the time the 1964 Conference/Convention rolled around, we were saturated with seriousness. "Let's have some fun," we urged one another. "We can start with our Convention."

The open-sharing session after the end of our first Conference in 1962 was the forerunner of all Conventions to come, and each year that session was expanded to include more activities.

In our festive mood, as we planned the 1964 Convention, we decided to add a dinner gathering before the evening's panel discussion. We were feeling our way; we didn't have much money, and we certainly didn't have experience in these matters. We had set up a panel with twelve members, each discussing one of the Twelve Steps and how it applied in his or her daily life.

I felt we needed to brighten things a bit, so we asked Esther G., our loyal GSO volunteer and non-professional comic, to provide a humorous introduction for the dinner.

As Jean S. remembered the occasion, "It was in my first year, and there was to be an affair with dinner and entertainment. My sisters, Doris and Lee, and our husbands went to this affair. And we expected to have a tremendous occasion. [Instead] we walked into this place, and it was mediocre. The entertainment, which we came to see, was only for five minutes. Esther was absolutely the most fabulous entertainment that we'd had, but it was only a few minutes, and then it was over.

"The family was all disappointed. I felt that I needed to involve myself in each affair. So after that night I talked to different people about what we could do for the next time."

As the result of Jean's dedicated efforts, Bebe F. volunteered to write and direct a play for the 1965 Convention, emphasizing various facets of the Twelve-Step program. With volunteer members as actors, singers and dancers, this was our first OA show, and it proved to be a resounding success.

For sixteen years our annual Convention was held immediately following the Business Conference. At most Conventions, the grand finale was a home-grown musical, continuing the tradition begun at the 1965 Convention. Eventually the whole arrangement became unwieldy as OA continued its rapid growth.

It became obvious that we needed to hold the Business Conference and the Convention separately. On November 29, 1976, the Board of Trustees moved that "beginning the third weekend of September, 1978, the annual World Service Convention site be rotated from region to region. . . ." (More about regions in Chapter Sixteen.)

"That's wonderful," we told each other. "It gives us more time for sharing and fellowship!" In 1978 the first stand-alone Convention was held in Kansas City, Missouri. Many later Conventions would be enhanced with singing and dancing, a practice that spread to other OA events as well.

That first OA musical in 1965 was the inspiration for all the shows to follow. At Conventions and assemblies and OA birthday celebrations, talented OA writers, directors, lyricists, musicians, singers, dancers and volunteer helpers created magnificent stories to entertain us all.

In fact, I joined in by writing a musical for the 1968 Convention, using original lyrics and familiar music. Emboldened by the warm response, the following year I wrote a two-hour musical history of OA called "The Caring Tie." This time I wrote both the story and the lyrics, using popular music. The show was produced at the 1969 Convention and repeated for the delegates at the 1979 Convention. Then it was put on by New York members during their 1980 gathering.

Ever since that first 1965 musical, OA members have been singing and dancing their way to recovery in shows all around the world. Their happiness is contagious.

When the house lights dim and the stage lights brighten, for a brief time our everyday problems disappear. We can hum along with the music while we smile and applaud together.

From the experience of these shows, we learn that recovery promises more than just a return to sanity and freedom from the bondage of food; it also includes enthusiasm and laughter. Each moment, each day becomes precious as we experience the irresistible joy of living!

Chapter Eleven

Abstinence and the Carbohydrate Controversy

URING the months that followed our first Conference and mini-Convention, I busied myself with the necessary follow-up work. So engrossed was I with the office (not to mention family, home and laundry) that I failed to notice the rumblings of discontent growing ever louder in our local Fellowship.

Finally, after a series of agitated phone calls from members in both Los Angeles and Valley groups, I began to give serious thought to our newest controversy. It had to do with the difference between a low-carbohydrate eating plan and abstinence from compulsive overeating.

During OA's earliest days, many of us counted calories in order to control our food intake. We'd grown up with that method; it was the dieter's mainstay. We'd been taught that as long as we stayed within our total daily allotment, we could eat all the low-calorie foods we wanted between meals. And we did just that! By mid-1961, many of us in OA had lost weight, but even more were nibbling their way back to obesity. Others were sticking with their diets but crunching all day on low-cal foods. Many just remained fat, rationalizing that they were only eating allowable foods between meals.

We had begun to see that all this nonstop "nibbling," even on carrots and celery, only increased our compulsion. It was keeping us focused on food and standing in the way of our recovery. Something crucial was missing from OA. What was it?

Although I'm not an alcoholic, during those early years I was attending AA meetings every week in order to learn more about the Twelve Steps and Twelve Traditions. From my first visit to Gamblers Anonymous in 1958, it had been clear to me that we compulsive overeaters had much in common with compulsive gamblers and alcoholics.

As I read the AA literature and listened to AA speakers, it was easy for me to "translate" their words to fit our situation. The real sticking point for all of us was AA's concept of sobriety. How does the compulsive overeater become sober? What did it mean for us to stop eating compulsively? Each OA member had a different interpretation, and we argued about this incessantly. We couldn't just "put the plug in the jug," as our AA friends constantly reminded us.

In the earliest OA meetings we shared techniques for "sticking with our diets." I can't recollect the word "abstinence" being used in those days, although it does appear in a list of "our working tools," compiled in August, 1961, for the original West Los Angeles OA group:

1. attend the meetings each week religiously
2. phoning
3. stripping the home of foods that help nourish a binge
4. have a calorie chart . . . count calories and measure
5. plan—think and prepare your course—3 meals a day
6. abstinence—do not eat between meals
7. make small goals
8. one day at a time, postpone, one hour at a time
9. read program at home—educate yourself with literature about nutrition

I don't remember the discussion surrounding this list, but I do recall clearly the day I came to believe that abstinence was the missing key to our physical recovery.

It was in late 1961 when I attended a powerful Sunday noon AA meeting that transformed my way of thinking about eating. Ordinarily, the AA's talked about sobriety. However, on this day the main speaker kept referring to "abstinence" from alcohol. The AA's who followed him talked about abstinence as well. This was the first time I'd ever heard sobriety referred to in that manner. It was a revelation!

Sitting in the back of that meeting, I thought to myself, "That's what's wrong with all of us in OA. We're not abstaining from food at any time during the day. We have to close our mouths from the end of one meal to the beginning of the next; otherwise, we're feeding our obsession."

Excitedly, I brought this approach to the next OA meeting. "Listen, everybody," I bubbled, "I have a great idea." I told them about the AA meeting and then informed them, "The word 'abstain' comes from the Greek, and it means 'to stay away from.' With our between-meal nibbling, we're not abstaining at all. In fact, we're eating all the time, even though we're counting calories." Some members thought it was an inspiration; others just laughed. But I wouldn't give up.

I believed the word would mean the same thing to the overeater that sobriety meant to the alcoholic. All we had to do was give a clear definition of what it means to abstain from eating compulsively.

In May, 1962, I set out to provide that clear definition. When I sat down to write our first *OA Bulletin* (described in detail in Chapter Four), I decided to introduce the concept of abstinence along with other OA news and information.

On page 3 of that first *Bulletin* I said:

> Out of our regular visits to AA meetings and talks with our friends in Alcoholics Anonymous, we here in the Los Angeles area have discovered a concept that has revolutionized our way of thinking about our compulsive overeating.
>
> That concept is "ABSTINENCE."
>
> Abstinence means simply three moderate meals a day with absolutely nothing in between. It means also no "meals" while we're preparing a meal and no "meals" while we're cleaning up the kitchen afterward. In other words, total abstinence from compulsive eating!
>
> If for medical reasons our doctor has ordered more than three meals a day, then of course we would plan accordingly and know that anything outside that plan would be breaking

abstinence. Of course, black coffee, tea, water, non-caloric beverages of any kind are the exception to between-meal nibbling.

Just as the alcoholic must totally abstain from alcohol to remain sober, so we have found we must totally abstain from compulsive eating to maintain our own kind of sobriety. We call those who have achieved this kind of sobriety "abstainers."

There are no "musts" to any part of the OA Program . . . indeed our Twelve Step Program is only a suggested plan for recovery. Therefore, we aren't saying that abstinence is a "must." We're only passing on to you what we have learned from our own experience . . . that with "abstinence" from compulsive eating we have at last found the true meaning of sobriety for the compulsive overeater.

I was a dietician's daughter, and all during my growing-up years my mother had drilled into me the importance of three meals a day. That's why I used that phrase in my new definition. I added the word "moderate," thinking that compulsive overeaters needed to be reminded to keep their portions reasonably small so that they would lose their excess weight and keep it off.

It never occurred to me that many overeaters had little understanding of moderation. For example, later on when we talked about "two pieces of chicken," some would rationalize that the right half and the left half of the chicken added up to two pieces. Others would insist that "two cups of lettuce" meant packing the greens down as firmly as possible while still fitting into a two-cup measure.

However, that day in May, 1962, as I reread my announcement before typing the *Bulletin* for mailing, my definition seemed so simple and so clear. I had no premonition of the controversy and confusion that would surround the word "abstinence" in the years to come.

In addition, another storm cloud was gathering just over the horizon.

In 1960, the *AA Grapevine* had published an unusual book to commemorate AA's twenty-fifth anniversary. The book was called *AA Today*, and it contained forty-four articles on a variety of AA-related subjects written by both AAs and their non-AA friends in medicine, politics, law, business, entertainment, the clergy and other professions.

One of these articles was to have a profound effect on Overeaters Anonymous for many decades.

Written by Father Edward J. Dowling, it was titled "AA Steps for the Underprivileged Non-AA":

> My 240-pound gluttony gave me two heart attacks. An alcoholic doctor got me down toward 180 [pounds] when he advised a total AA abstinence from starch, butter, salt and sugar. He said these four foods were probably my "alcohol." Abstinence was so much easier than temperance. The "balanced" diet often prescribed was loaded with the four "craving-creating appetizers." I was like a lush tapering off on martinis. Only after the discovery of the AA approach to craving-creating intake did I realize that the Jesuit Ignatius' first rule for diet in his Spiritual Exercises was to go easy on craving-creating food and drink.
>
> Reprinted by permission of Alcoholics Anonymous Grapevine, Inc.

In 1961, when Irene read Father Ed's story, she felt she had stumbled upon an important new idea. Even while she was crusading for the OA Twelve Steps to be restored to AA's Steps and for OA to become a primarily spiritual program, she also began developing another cause.

However, for at least a year she talked about her latest brainstorm only to her OA friend, Mildred J., a registered nurse. Together they were trying Irene's new way of eating before bringing it to the rest of us.

From Father Ed's paragraph about his gluttony, Irene decided that only flour and sugar were the overeater's "trigger foods," and she called them "refined carbohydrates." She felt salt and butter, although unwise and unhealthy, were not nearly as craving-creating.

By August, 1962, Mildred had lost seventy pounds. During the open-sharing session after our first Conference, she told us:

> I feel I have the allergy to carbohydrates, just as the alcoholic has the allergy to alcohol. . . . On my way down [in weight], I first cut out some carbohydrates, and then I would reach a plateau, and more would go, and more would go. I started by only cutting out the concentrated carbohydrates, and now I have gotten down to the place where I have practically none left. I have abstained a year and six days, and this truly is the easier, softer way that I was searching for all my life.
>
> I want to carry the message. I feel like going around to everyone and saying, 'Do you have a problem with your carbohydrates? I have the answer!'

At that point in OA's development, Mildred's speech had little impact on the rest of us. We were all involved in establishing Overeaters Anonymous on a firm, unified foundation. So much was happening that no one commented about her remarks for many months.

Meanwhile, unaware of Irene's activities regarding a low-carbohydrate eating plan, I was busy promoting my own concept of abstinence. While I thought my explanation was clear, others were confused.

One of these was A.G., the chairman of our new Board of Trustees. He and other Gluttons Anonymous members who came into OA from Texas spoke of "sticking to my diet" and "sobriety." As chairman, A.G. felt he needed to clearly define the word "abstinence" and how it would be used in the OA literature the board was developing. Therefore, on November 3, 1962, he sent a letter to all the trustees on the subject of abstinence:

> The dictionary definition is not of much importance here, since what we are actually doing is using an existing word to describe a feeling or state of being that is not in the vocabulary of the average person. . . . The word "abstinence" has become ambiguous in its development in the program since it means something to us when we use it and to the person that hears it the meaning is altered or modified to their understanding. . . . When someone from one of the California groups uses the word, I understand it to mean some or all of

the following things: Since there has been some disagreement about the Twelve Steps and how they should be written, abstinence has been applied to those who are working the AA Steps instead of modified or weakened Steps, or in this sense it means someone who is working the OA Steps and Traditions as agreed upon at the Conference. . . .

It can also mean someone who is not eating compulsively and doing so happily.

Possibly the most important meaning of 'abstinence' in California is its definition of a certain plan of eating, to wit: three planned meals a day with nothing in-between. This definition of the word, in my opinion, sets up 'rules,' something with which I very much disagree.

I am in agreement with all of these definitions except the latter, although I think we might find some other words that express these things more accurately, rather than have one term cover a variety of things.

Concerning the latter definition, the set of 'rules,' I feel that this is something that we not only should not do, but really have no right to do. This program is not designed as a diet plan, but as a way of life in which we can be relieved of the compulsion to eat one day at a time. . . .

This program is to give you a choice as to whether or not you want to follow whatever set of rules seems to fit you best. When you are obsessed with a compulsion to eat, you have no choice—working the program you have the power to choose and do what you want to, but the choice must still be made daily. I don't think any set of rules will make this choice any better or easier. I think a mandatory set of rules will make it more difficult rather than easier. . . .

As to a discussion of an eating plan, I feel that this is best done on a 12-Step call or in a discussion between a member and his sponsor. If we can tie the Twelve Steps and Traditions together along with sponsorship, I think we have eliminated the need for any set of rules, eating plan or otherwise.

Within a few weeks, A.G. received replies to his letter from all the trustees except Ethel. In my letter to him, I said:

As for your memo on abstinence, I think we have discussed that rather thoroughly. When I talk about it here, I usually use the entire phrase "abstinence from compulsive eating" rather than just abstinence alone. I also discuss three meals a day, OR WHATEVER WORKS BEST FOR THE INDIVIDUAL. Also a sensible calorie count and avoidance of the foods about which I am compulsive. I don't believe we are in disagreement at all; it was just a misunderstanding. Although we can always be definite about ourselves, such as "From my own experience I know that I can't eat such-and-such foods and that my mealtimes must be thus-and-so," nevertheless we try (at least I try) to put the burden of ultimate responsibility upon the individual and his own conscience. This way we set up no "rules," only explaining the lessons learned from our own experiences. Since there are no "musts" in O.A., I believe this is how the entire program should be presented. After all, even A.A. calls them Twelve <u>Suggested</u> Steps to Recovery.

As the holidays approached, I continued to busy myself with home, family and the ever-increasing OA office responsibilities.

Meanwhile, out in the Valley, Irene was becoming excited about her newest cause—abstinence from all refined carbohydrates. Those storm clouds I mentioned earlier loomed closer, threatening our newly-established harmony.

On January 10, 1963, Irene wrote to A.G.:

> I am getting my abstinence <u>for sure,</u> down pat. I have found there are other foods I must quit besides my binge foods. I feel I have finally found <u>my answer for me</u>. Here are the exact words from an A.A. Grapevine [publication] by an alcoholic priest.

Irene then proceeded to quote the paragraph from Father Edward Dowling's article in *AA Today*, provided earlier in this chapter. After the quote, Irene continued:

> A.G., I have a tremendous sense of excitement about this. Several of the girls have automatically cut the foods out of their diets and [are] going along very serene and happy.
>
> I can't help but wonder if overeaters with this kind of eating would not be as apt to slip. I wonder if we have an allergy of the body too. I know science has proved that some fat people can't handle carbohydrates, that it turns to fat in their

system, and all these foods come under the refined carbohydrate list. Are we going to help the Doctors understand obesity just as the alcoholic had to educate the medical profession?

Irene's discovery of Father Dowling's article had been the
catalyst for her development of a plan of eating which specifically excluded all foods high in carbohydrates. After a year
or so, during which she and Mildred lost weight, Irene was
ready to take on the rest of OA.

Her 1963 letter to A.G. was only the beginning. At first
she began to carry her particular message to members of the
Valley groups. "I have the solution for all of OA," she would
exclaim, clutching the *AA Today* book.

Eventually, she and Mildred drove over the hill to talk to
the members in some of the Los Angeles groups. She would
hold up her book and then expound upon her plan. Irene
had a powerful speaking manner and tremendous charisma,
and it wasn't long before she had won over some of the Los
Angeles members. Entranced by her presentation, they decided to embrace her way of eating.

Rosalind J., a Los Angeles member, recalls: "I came to my
first OA meeting in February, 1964. I heard Irene talk, and I
was saved! I felt as if I were home. Irene communicated to
you directly. She drew you in. I was drawn to her like a mag-
net, and she became my sponsor."

Bernice S. also reminisced: "I had moved to the Valley
and heard about OA in early 1963. My friend gave me Irene's
phone number. I called her, then hesitated and made excus-
es not to go, saying I couldn't get a babysitter. Irene said, 'I
have a teenage daughter who babysits for fifty cents an hour.
I'll bring her with me. I'm going to pick you up tonight and
take you to the meeting at Shadow Ranch Park.'"

Bernice continued, "Irene was a very loving person who
cared deeply about the people she sponsored. Her big thing
was her eating plan, weighing and measuring, and working
the Twelve Steps. She forbade me to go over the hill to a
meeting in Los Angeles. I never even knew for my first year
that I was in this program that there were some other people

over the hill that didn't eat on the gold sheet [Irene's food plan]."

As Irene tried to force her eating plan on everyone else in OA, controversy escalated. The phone lines heated up as anguished calls went back and forth.

Irene had written her eating plan without consulting anyone in the field of nutrition. Because of my mother's early nutritional training, I immediately recognized that this diet didn't include grains, one of the four basic food groups. I was worried when many members began touting Irene's plan as the only way to eat. "What if someone becomes ill and blames OA?" I asked. "Would they sue us?" I was told not to worry because Mildred had medical expertise; she was a nurse. Nevertheless, I refused to print that eating plan without the approval of the Conference delegates.

Circumventing the OA printing procedure, Irene took the approach she'd used two years earlier with the booklets she'd found at AA meetings. She simply printed the food plans herself, copyrighted them under her husband's name and sold them at "her" groups.

The first low-carbohydrate eating plan was published on gold paper, and members called it the "gold sheet." It was a simple five-by-seven-inch card. On one side it stated:

> We compulsive over-eaters feel that we are addicted to refined carbohydrates. We suggest this abstinence, which our experience, and the experience of others, have found successful. REMEMBER!! Honesty and self-discipline are the keys to recovery.

Then it gave further information for measuring food, food preparation and foods we avoid. On the other side of the card were suggested menus and permissible foods listed under various food groups. Most important were the four statements at the top of that page:

> 1. We eat 3 meals a day, nothing in-between except black coffee, plain tea or no-cal drinks. 2. We abstain completely from any refined carbohydrates, and any natural carbohy-

drates above 10 percent. 3. We abstain from second helpings at our meals. 4. We suggest that you do NOT skip meals.

I remember violent arguments over Irene's insistence that we could not have any lemon juice in our tea or cream in our coffee between meals. That was a constant bone of contention between the "carbohydrate abstainers" and the "three-moderate-mealers."

In addition, Irene said she had read in William James' book, *Varieties of Religious Experience*, that it took twenty-one days to break a habit. She insisted all meeting speakers had to have three weeks of abstinence. Eventually, that requirement became thirty days. As time went on, she also declared that all speakers had to have given away a Fourth-Step inventory.

Irene had been exposed to AA before she'd heard about OA. She believed strongly that the Twelve Steps were vital to a healthy life. Convinced of her allergy to sugar and flour, she linked her eating plan to the Twelve Steps. "You can't work one element without the other," she proclaimed.

Maxine R., who was sponsored by Irene in 1963 and 1964, said years later, "Irene was very positive. She had the power of persuasion. She said to me, 'If you eat this way and work these Twelve Steps, I guarantee you'll lose the compulsion to overeat and live a spiritual life.' I said, 'Yea! Yea! Gimme some of that!' And I started to eat that way; I started to abstain that way."

Other members shared Irene's and Mildred's missionary zeal for carbohydrate abstinence. They began to talk about it and write letters to our new little *OA Bulletin*. In the December, 1963, issue, the following editorial comment appeared:

> Among the responses [to the earlier *Bulletin*] were a number representing one group. These letters, among other things of interest, expressed the view that 'man-made' carbohydrates are compulsion inciting, and that abstention from such carbohydrates is mandatory to the successful maintenance of food control.

The writer of the editorial, who was probably Ethel K., went on to say:

> Since we deal with a subject so largely neglected by science, . . . it seems only right that the Bulletin be a forum for all points of view. There are undoubtedly as many approaches to the problem of compulsive overeating as there are compulsive overeaters. . . . But perhaps it should be borne in mind that it is not an indicated concern of O.A. in general to deal with individual techniques of achieving non-compulsiveness in the area of food itself.

Irene persisted in printing her gold sheet, copyrighted under her husband's name. In 1964 she continued that copyright on green paper, which we then called the "green sheet."

As Maxine recalled: "The copyright was to protect the sheet. Irene was a smart lady. She knew that if other groups started to print it, they would add this or take that away or they'd change it, and she didn't want it changed. She wanted it her way. I really think she felt she had found the 'cure.' She was sincere about it. And she was very definite about not having anybody change or alter that plan in any way, because she felt that that's the way it should stand.

"It wasn't called 'gray sheet' yet," Maxine went on. "It was printed on every color under the rainbow . . . whatever color paper we could get that was cheapest at the time."

In the minutes of the 1964 OA Conference, members referred to the plan as the "green sheet." The women who followed it called themselves "carbohydrate abstainers" or "carbohydrate girls."

"At the same time," Maxine said, "Irene was the one who started talking about going to AA and working the Steps. And I started going to meetings at the Palms Hotel at Third and Alvarado. Irene was like a strong mother figure. She was very definite about her ideas and believed in what she was doing. She was good for me. She was the first person who said to me, 'You will not recover in this program unless you work the Steps.' And she said, 'The place to learn to work the Steps is in AA.' And she sent me to APOAR as well as AA."

APOAR, which stood for Applied Principles of Alcoholic Recovery, was a separate organization. It had been started for those AA members who weren't succeeding in AA. It had its own book and offered a very structured approach to working the Twelve Steps.

"So a group of us used to go down there every week to that hotel," Maxine recalled, "and listen to the way to work the program. I read the book and got started working the Steps. And that's when I did my first [Fourth-Step] inventory—in 1964. I went to APOAR for six or eight months, and then we started our own OA group, the Van Nuys Wednesday night group, in April of 1964."

Until that time, the Valley groups had been a mixture of "regular OA" and "carbohydrate OA." But this new group, begun by Maxine and JoAnne P., was OA's first group exclusively for people who were following the low-carbohydrate eating plan.

Only those who were carbohydrate abstainers with at least thirty days on that food plan could share at the Van Nuys meeting. In addition, all speakers had to have given away their Fourth-Step inventory. The concept proved immediately popular.

Maxine remembered, "At first we met in JoAnne's living room. After four months, the room was packed and people were hanging out the door. So we moved to Van Nuys Park, and often there were one hundred people at the meeting. It was the carbohydrate abstinence that brought them in in such large numbers."

By late 1964 many people had lost weight with the new plan and the Twelve Steps. The Van Nuys Park group decided to institute a slightly different eating plan for those lucky members. Although still very low-carbohydrate, it was called "Carbohydrate Maintaining Abstinence." Stapled to it was a little disclaimer sheet which read:

> One of the Overeaters Anonymous Low Carbohydrate Groups has printed this Maintaining Abstinence Sheet as a guide to members who have lost all of their excess weight

and who are maintaining their normal weight. This sheet does not represent the endorsement of Overeaters Anonymous as a whole. It is not to be used by those who have not lost all of their weight.

This plan was not copyrighted by Irene or anyone else. The portions were slightly larger than on the green sheet, and more foods had been added.

However, not everyone in OA agreed with Irene's insistence that we were all allergic to sugar and refined carbohydrates. The controversy continued to grow.

I overreacted, too. I felt so threatened by Irene that I refused to hear anything she said. I believed she was trying to corrupt my original concept of Overeaters Anonymous, which was simply a Twelve-Step recovery program for compulsive overeaters without any specific eating plan. In retrospect, I feared she would take OA away from me and make it "her" organization.

At the same time, I wasn't the only one resisting the imposition of the carbohydrate eating plan. Many OA members, both in the Valley groups and in Los Angeles, insisted that an eating plan should be up to the individual. They refused to accept Irene's precepts. There were terrible fights and name-calling. The "carbohydrate girls" called any groups which didn't agree with them the "fat-serenity groups." It didn't even matter if a member had lost all her excess weight. If she didn't eat according to Irene's plan, she was still said to be rationalizing "fat serenity."

In the beginning I'd hoped that this carbohydrate abstinence was just a passing fad. Alas, I was living in a dreamer's paradise. I didn't recognize the compulsive overeater's need to hang on to a rigid eating plan, just the way we had surrendered to our diets in our pre-OA days.

One of Irene's positive contributions was her insistence on the importance of working the Twelve Steps. Even her advocacy of eating only three meals a day was in line with all the other OA groups. Unfortunately, these constructive practices were lost in her trumpeting of the carbohydrate allergy.

Mildred, her staunchest supporter, had such a sweet voice and a gentle, beautiful smile. I can remember hearing her say, "Sugar turns to alcohol in our bodies. When we eat sugar, our bodies become veritable stills, like the old-time moonshiners."

I was so taken aback by her statement that I never did challenge her or ask her where she got her facts. In retrospect, it probably wouldn't have done any good. Mildred was so spellbound by Irene and her beliefs that she would have stuck to her statement, no matter what. "Remember," she used to remind us, "I've lost seventy pounds with this way of eating." Who could argue with success?

During the Board of Trustees meeting on October 19, 1963, A.G. appointed Irene, along with Carol and Thelma, "to take care of preliminary Convention arrangements, committee appointments, . . . and to send a printed program of the scheduled events to all groups." At that point Irene was still very active as an OA trustee, but sometime in early spring of 1964, her attitude began to change. Incredibly, she was thinking of leaving the Fellowship. In looking back, it appears she was just waiting for the results of the Conference to finalize her decision one way or the other.

OA's Board of Trustees and we in the traditional OA groups had watched the phenomenal growth of the "carbohydrate" meetings with growing frustration and alarm. I remember tremendous agitation among the members that spring of 1964. The phone lines sizzled with reports and rumors about what was going on in the Valley. Everybody was preparing to confront the issue at the May Conference. Thelma wrote to A.G. on April 1, 1964:

> A.G., I'd like to ask a favor, . . . would you please include in your opening speech what you included last year? Everyone has a right to their own conception of a Higher Power, to their own conception of abstinence, and to their own conception of what is normal weight for them. . . .
>
> It is unbelieveable what is happening out here, and there are people in OA who don't know this is so.

Unfortunately, their delegates refuse to tell certain groups there is more than one conception. As far as they are concerned, those who don't go along with their thinking are "drunk". . . . And they refuse to let people like me speak at their meetings, or even get up and announce an A.A. speaker for another type group. . . .

They tell newcomers flatly, "Do not go to other groups. They'll only confuse you." Newcomers are given a diet to follow, and if they don't adhere strictly to this diet, they've broken their diet—or abstinence. If they complain that it's too rigid, and that they have a way of their own that loses weight, or that their doctor has them on a certain type diet, they are told, "You don't need us. Go to one of the fat serenity groups" or "You don't need OA. Go to your doctor."

From his neutral home base in Texas, A.G. worked valiantly to keep OA from falling apart due to the raging carbohydrate war in California. However, when he arrived for the third National Conference in May of 1964, he walked right into the middle of a pitched battle.

Irene had been on the Conference planning committee, but she had recently resigned as trustee and was not at the Conference. She turned her crusade over to Mildred, Maxine and the other carbohydrate abstainers.

Very early in the Conference discussion, A.G. brought up his own problems with the carbohydrate abstainers, saying, "It has been expressed that those who were not using carbohydrate abstinence were wrong and that they were cheating and that they were being dishonest. This has been expressed to me personally."

Gene S. from Northern California was furious at what he'd heard about membership requirements at the carbohydrate meetings. "If I attended that group on carbohydrates," he demanded to know, "would I be allowed to get up and speak if I wasn't on carbohydrate abstinence?"

Bernice S., a carbohydrate abstainer from the Valley jumped up. "Yes!" she declared. "In my group that I lead, you would be allowed to speak only if you were abstaining. Because I don't want a drunk up there talking. I don't care if you are on a carbohydrate abstinence or something else. You could speak as long as you were losing and had your abstinence."

Thelma pointedly asked Bernice, "A speaker doesn't have to be a carbohydrate abstainer in your group, but is this true of all carbohydrate groups?" Bernice admitted, "No, it is not."

Tempers were rising in the room. Miriam S., a delegate from Los Angeles, stood up. "I'm an abstainer," Miriam said. "I've been an abstainer since I entered the program. I've lost seventy-two pounds. I was at a carbohydrate group, and when they said, 'would abstainers speak,' I got up to speak. I was cut in the middle of what I was going to say because, number one, I did not give my weight, and number two, because I did not abstain according to the green sheet."

"Well, I've never seen anything like it," Gene burst out, "when they won't let a person get up and speak because they're not on carbohydrate abstinence! It's going against all principles of OA." Gene, who had been in AA for twelve years, was also distressed over the misuse of the word "drunk." He objected to that frequently.

Shirley D., from the Northridge Valley group, spoke about the specific Traditions she felt were being violated, namely Traditions Two and Four. "When people are turned away from meetings in the name of OA, this is affecting OA as a whole, and the statements are made, people are cut off, as Miriam said . . . and people are told, 'you do not belong here.'"

Another delegate objected to a misuse of medical and nutritional terminology by the carbohydrate abstainers. "These people who are talking about carbohydrate abstinence," she insisted, "really have no idea how foods are assimilated, what foods consist of. All foods are converted to sugar when they get into your system. . . . You say a person is 'drunk' from eating some of these foods, but all foods break down into sugar anyway. What do we do? Only drink water?"

Mildred stood up. Speaking softly and deliberately, she said, "I'm a carbohydrate girl, and I think there's a lot of things we could say about the program that nobody really understands. Speaking for the groups that I go to, we have been united, and one of the reasons we are united is that we have a common solution, and it is the Twelve Steps. Also, we found we are people who have to eat alike, and there is more strength and power in having that [common bond of] both the Twelve Steps and the eating. This is our policy. We have gotten together and we set this policy. . . . And this is what we say when we open our meetings, 'Will those of you who care to, share your experience with carbohydrate abstinence.' Because this is what we are.

"Anyone is welcome to come [to our meetings]. I don't see how anyone could say that I was judging or imposing if they are welcome to come to the meeting."

Thelma had an objection to this reasoning: "This is a program of giving," she said. "I get in accordance with the way I give, so of what value, then, is it for me to go to a meeting where I can't give? I get nothing."

Mildred lifted her chin. "Yes, I can see that it looks like this is the time for separation," she said. "This is all I can say. You have a place to give, and I have my place to give, and perhaps this is the answer."

As Mildred finished speaking, my heart sank. I sat at the front table looking out over the crowded room. I couldn't believe my ears. "What's happening here?" I asked myself. "Is this the end of OA?" I wanted to cry. All that time and effort, all my hopes and dreams. Were they to be dashed forever? Would one faction or the other walk out of the Conference and withdraw from OA? It seemed on the verge of happening, but instead, the delegates turned out to be more interested in continuing the argument. (Perhaps this has been OA's saving grace all along. We'd rather fight than switch!)

The discussion dragged on and on. It spilled into the hallways during breaks. Anger and resentment inflamed the proceedings, although A.G. and other cooler heads continually tried to put out the fires.

Finally, I could stand it no longer; my beloved Overeaters

Anonymous was being torn to pieces. I felt very strongly then (and still do) about the issue of suffering compulsive overeaters being made to feel unwelcome at OA meetings. My hands were shaking as I rose to speak. "I want to say something about what what has been said here," I began. "A meeting can be closed [to some overeaters] by implication, without saying it. We are all here because we have a haven in OA, and for one overeater to make another overeater feel guilty or ashamed is the greatest tragedy of all. We have nobody but each other and no place to go but here, and if we make one another feel, in any way, the way we felt in the outer world, we have destroyed what we believe in and defeated our own purpose. And I think we all need to consider a little more compassion in our attitudes."

After more arguing, Gene had had enough. "I make a motion," he urged, "that we move on to new or old business."

A.G. asked for discussion on the motion, and the delegates started in again. There was more mud-throwing, more retaliation on both sides. A.G. tried to take control and restore order.

Then Wally M. jumped up. "What it seems like to me is that there's more than one way of accomplishing the results that OA as a whole is wanting, since each group is autonomous. We could go on talking and arguing the various ways all day long, so let's have a vote and go on to something else."

A.G. took advantage of the resulting silence. "All those in favor of ending this discussion," he said, "raise their right hand. All opposed? I believe it carries unanimously."

Of course, nothing was settled, and I could see that no minds were really changed. The "regular OA" faction was in the majority at this Convention. Therefore, when we had elections for new trustees, Maxine was defeated by Lorene of Arizona. We weren't ready yet for a carbohydrate abstainer on our board, but that day wasn't too far off.

After treasurer's and General Service Office reports, we

had discussions on national publicity, literature, expense reimbursements and the fate of the *OA Bulletin.*

Finally, the 1964 Third Annual OA Conference ended without any real meeting of the minds between the carbohydrate abstainers and the "regular OA" delegates. OA had managed to hang together, but just barely.

Bernice remembers, "When Irene heard that no action had been taken on adopting her eating plan for OA, she was fed up. And she simply walked out [of OA]."

According to Maxine, "She might have felt she was beating her head against a wall. Maybe she was just ready to go on to something else. I wanted to leave OA with Irene. I have no idea where we were going to go, but whatever she was going to do, I wanted to go do it with her. And she said, 'No, you need to stay here, you need to be the keeper of this plan.' So Irene endowed me with the copyright for the green sheet. 'I entrust you with seeing that nobody bastardizes this sheet,' she told me. And so, in the early days nobody could print that sheet but our group, under my direction. Anyone who wanted a copy of the sheet had to come to Van Nuys and buy it there. That's how it was. We sold it at what it cost us. We never made any money on it."

Maxine continued, "It was printed on a single sheet of paper at first; then I made it into a folded card. Irene would not allow OA to say 'Go see your doctor before you use this plan.' She refused to have that printed on the sheet. She felt that it canceled out the validity of it. But we felt that it was necessary after Irene left. We had discussions in the Wednesday night Van Nuys group that we could be held responsible if anybody got sick, so we were going to have a stamp made and stamp it on the sheet. But then we were afraid that if she saw that, she would pull the sheet. So we had it printed on little pieces of paper and slipped it in with the plan. And people would say 'Oh, look at that,' and toss the piece of paper out."

Maxine also recalled, "We used to print sponsors' phone

numbers on the front of the sheet. It said, 'Any questions call,' and there used to be half a dozen names of sponsors."

Meanwhile, right after the Conference, A.G. wrote to the trustees:

> I have been pleased to learn that those in our fellowship that are practicing carbohydrate abstinence have decided that their place is in OA, with just a very few exceptions. I really believe that the solution to most of the problems that confront us today is to be found in growth, individually and as a whole. There will always be some who think that since a particular thing has worked for them, it is the ONLY way. Taking into the account the personality that most of us had when we began, this is not too surprising. As long as our unity is based only on the 12 Steps and 12 Traditions, and each of us practice them to the best of our ability, differences and controversies will be handled by our Higher Power.

The Conference had taken all of my free time, and when it was over, my husband and two little girls welcomed Mommy home, hoping for undivided attention. I did my best, cooking for the family, participating in parents' events at school, doing the family laundry, even going out with Marvin for fun! However, every night from 7:30 to midnight I kept up with OA office work. It was definitely a full schedule.

On June 19, 1964, I wrote to A.G.:

> The carbohydrate thing only <u>seems</u> to have simmered down here; in reality they have sort of gone underground. Irene, Mildred, Nora and another girl have withdrawn from OA and have formed a little group called Carbohydrates Addicts. I understand they use the Twelve Steps but not the Twelve Traditions. However, the OA-carbohydrates groups are now using a little yellow sheet (instead of the green diet sheet). I haven't seen it, but someone told me it is stamped "copyright 1963 by Frank B____," who is Irene's husband. My own feeling is just to let them alone and not react so much. I think this whole thing will die a natural death when they find out they need the Presence of God more than the absence of carbohydrates.

On July 11 A.G. wrote to me:

> I have a copy of the yellow sheet you mentioned. The Carbohydrate groups are using it, and it is not copyrighted by B____, but by Roberts Publishing Company, P.O. Box 2063, Alhambra, California. It is simply a listing of various foods, which I assume they use as I use a calorie counter.

(To set the record straight, Irene's first "gold sheet" was printed "copyright Merrill C. B____." He was Irene's husband. Then in 1965, after she had left OA, the plan was printed on various paper colors, mostly white, and read "copyright 1965 I. B____." Finally, her sheet was done on yellow paper and read "copyright 1967 I. B____.")

In July, 1964, when Lorene decided she was unable to serve on the board, A.G. wrote to the trustees:

> I wonder if we could elect another trustee by mail so that the new member could attend the October meeting? In my opinion, it would be best if we could elect the person who ran second on the ballot that elected Lorene. . . .

Of course, this would be Irene's heir apparent, Miss Carbohydrate herself, Maxine R! (Three decades later, Maxine and I would laugh together at this title.)

That same month, in a separate letter to me, A.G. said,

> I don't know how the rest of them will feel about the method of selecting the new trustee, but I privately hope that it comes out with a member of one of the carbohydrate groups as the one selected so they will have some representation on the Board.

Horrified by his suggestion, I answered,

> I must disagree with you about the carbohydrate member. Honestly, A.G., it's rather sad. They are still so dogmatic. They unbooked, as it were, one of the members who eats that way but doesn't believe that's the <u>only</u> way to eat. Unfortunately, the group I go to voted not to have carbohydrate speakers because they are so darn pushy on the subject. Then, another member started a group in Santa Monica and approached a carbohydrate member asking her for help. The woman said that if the group were turned into a carbohydrate

group, they could have all the help they wanted, many speakers and leaders, etc. But if they didn't want to go the carbohydrate way, then Fran was told they could all go flounder on their own. Now, I still feel that time and God will take care of all of us, but in the meantime, their attitude is still very sad and not the OA way at all. I have really let go of this and try very hard not to become involved in any discussions or controversy. But please, no carbohydrate member on the Board of Trustees. It's bad enough that Maxine, who is their new leader, is the Treasurer [of OA]. Would you have Castro run for Vice-President? I cannot publicly give the OA stamp of approval to the fact that this is the <u>only</u> way to abstain from overeating, and I don't believe you go along with this theory either.

Thelma was even more upset by this suggestion than I was. On July 20, 1964, she wrote to A.G.:

Honestly, A.G.,I have no objections to anyone just because they abstain from refined carbohydrates. I can only point out that Section 8.7a says that it is the duty of the trustees to act as guardians of the Twelve Steps and the Twelve Traditions.

I am not concerned with the way they eat, only with the way they operate. Can they guard what they don't maintain?

If I lived in the Van Nuys area and was compelled to go to the V.N. group, let's say, because I couldn't get it elsewhere, I would be given a "gold" sheet, the one Irene is presently using in her "Carbohydrate Addicts" group. I would be told that this is the way they eat in their group, and any other way is not abstaining. I would be instructed that the first step to honesty is to tell what I weigh and whether or not I had lost. I would be given a choice of picking a sponsor from four girls, Maxine R., Marion G., JoAnne P. and someone named Connie. I would have to report to them daily exactly what I had eaten, and if it so happened that I didn't stick exactly to that gold sheet, I would be punished by not being allowed to call my sponsor for three days. This, even if I had lost weight!

In two or three weeks I would have to make moral inventory, whether or not I was ready, and it would have to be with "the" sponsor. Talk about "musts"! They use the "APOAR" textbook, also "Body, Mind and Sugar" and the Twelve Steps as their guides. The only Tradition they observe is the Fourth, which says they have the right to be wrong. They don't give the same right to their members or to other OA members.

Since Irene, Mildred and Nora left OA, Maxine is now literally their high priestess and their authority, and Marion is her disciple. I cannot vote for someone when I know they do not maintain the Traditions. According to Section 2.1, even a delegate is supposed to do that.

They announce clearly and positively, "Do not talk here unless you have carbohydrate abstinence." Any OA group that will not allow OA members to share their experience, strength and hope unless they eat a certain way is not contributing to the unity of OA as a whole. That is the opinion of the majority of OAs out here. It is also my opinion.

As things turned out, Mabel S. of North Hollywood was appointed trustee to fill out Lorene's term. Maxine continued to serve as OA's national treasurer (as she would do until early 1976).

By 1966, the carbohydrate abstainers were represented at Conference in greater numbers, and Maxine was elected a trustee, the first carbohydrate abstainer to serve on the board. In May, 1969, she was elected chairman of the board, and she served in that capacity until May, 1970.

Whatever happened to Irene? She seemed to have dropped out of sight. The mystery was solved in a letter from Thelma to A.G. dated July 10, 1967:

> Grace R. from Petaluma is here . . . and I fixed her lunch. Also had Mabel, Irene and Mildred. They all look great . . . all except Irene are in OA. . . . For a while she turned to Science of Mind and became a practitioner, but she said her inner conflicts were such that she had to go back to Christian Science, and the practitioner who is working with her says she must give up everything, including OA and AA and not even talk about them any more.

Although we never saw Irene in OA again, the heated discussions about food plans continued during the annual National Conference in May, 1965. By that time the letter

158

praising OA had run in Dear Abby's column, and our tiny office staff had been overwhelmed with pleas for help.

As the carbohydrate controversy continued unabated through 1965, we all realized we had to find a common ground if we were to help ourselves and the seven thousand who had written to us in response to Abby's column.

In November, 1965, a notice was sent to all groups by Margaret P., our National Executive Secretary. It was titled:

OVEREATERS ANONYMOUS—
FIRST INTER-GROUP MEETINGS

It called for two meetings of all groups in the greater Los Angeles area. The first meeting was to be held in Los Angeles, the second "on the Valley side."

(Although intergroups weren't officially established until the early 1970's, this was the first time the phrase had been used. It was a promising forecast of our future.)

On February 17, 1966, representatives from more than twenty groups met at the Episcopal Church on Olympic Boulevard in Los Angeles. The delegates began by talking about love, understanding and responsibility towards one another and to the group. Breathing a sigh of relief, I felt it was a hopeful beginning.

As the night wore on, however, the low-carbohydrate advocates continued to push their cause. Others pleaded for reason and sanity. At the time it seemed to be a continuation of the unfortunate argument during the 1964 Conference. I do remember suggesting that we use the phrase "starches and sweets" in place of "refined carbohydrates," and that suggestion met with unanimous approval.

However, three decades later, while listening to the tapes of that intergroup meeting, it became apparent to me that we had been slowly shifting from overreacting to the personalities of the low-carbohydrate supporters to exploring the principles involved in the disagreements. Should OA have one eating plan? If so, what plan should we print? Would a food-plan endorsement still fall within the scope of the Twelve Traditions, or would it become an "outside issue"?

Although it was a three-hour discussion, we couldn't reach agreement on answers to these questions at that little 1966 intergroup meeting, and we never did hold the second, follow-up get-together. The eating-plan problem would continue to plague OA for several decades as we tried one solution after another.

In the meantime, the flood of responses to Dear Abby's column and the dramatic increase in OA groups pushed me to draft a new pamphlet. I wanted to give all those newcomers a general set of guidelines about abstinence, without directing them to eat specific foods.

I brought my proposal to the Board of Trustees. The minutes of the trustees' meeting on February 26, 1966, state: "The Board asked Rozanne to submit a draft of *OA Questions and Answers on Abstinence* and another OA pamphlet."

After input from the trustees, I wrote one pamphlet entitled *To The Newcomer.* The inside front cover gave a definition of abstinence:

> Abstinence in Overeaters Anonymous means abstinence from compulsive overeating. An eating plan is the method by which we abstain. The following is our suggested method of abstinence from compulsive overeating.
> 1. THREE MODERATE MEALS A DAY WITH NOTHING IN-BETWEEN BUT LOW- OR NO-CALORIE BEVERAGES.
> 2. AVOIDANCE OF ALL INDIVIDUAL BINGE FOODS.
>
> Overeaters Anonymous does not endorse any particular eating plan. Before making any change in your way of eating—and particularly if you have a specific medical problem—we suggest you see your doctor to decide upon the plan best suited to your physical needs.

The next two pages described the miracle of OA and the hope we offered to the compulsive overeater.

After that came sections describing our three levels of recovery—emotional, spiritual and physical. Four pages followed under a general title, "About Abstinence from

Compulsive Overeating." These pages included sections called "Three Moderate Meals a Day with Nothing In-between But Low- or No-Calorie Beverages," "Moderation," "Starches and Sweets," "Avoid Skipping Meals or Second Helpings," "Just For Today," "Telephone Calls" and "The Twelve Steps and Twelve Traditions." The final section gave a brief history of OA.

The pamphlet was finished in time to present to the delegates at the fifth annual National Conference in May, 1966. (This was the only time proposed OA literature was edited by the delegates on the Conference floor, comma by comma and paragraph by paragraph!) After discussing all the changes, the delegates approved *To The Newcomer* for publication. Overeaters Anonymous was growing very fast during the last half of the 1960s, spurred on by the 1965 letter in Dear Abby's column. The carbohydrate groups, such as the Wednesday night Van Nuys meeting, were growing faster than the "regular OA" groups.

At the same time, many of the original trustees, including A.G., Sonny, Thelma and me, had experienced relapse and were struggling to return to abstinence.

Irene's original food plan continued to be printed by Maxine and the Valley groups on various colored papers. Sometime during the late 1960s, they settled on gray paper, and the low-carbohydrate food plan came to be known as the "Gray Sheet." I was still upset by the lack of balance in their way of eating, and I never stopped advocating a second plan.

The disagreements over the "right way" to eat continued among the OA members. Natalie B. describes an occurrence during the 1974 Convention:

> It happened in one of the marathons. Remember that Gray Sheet allowed two pieces of chicken. Someone said that chewing on the bones added more pieces. Another member opposed that view, and the argument began. Finally, after an agitated discussion, the consensus was that the bones were 'inside' the chicken and therefore could be counted among

the original pieces. 'Don't feel guilty for chewing on the bones,' the majority triumphantly ruled!

Despite the various points of view, by the early 1970s others besides myself were beginning to realize that we needed to offer more than one method of eating so that our members would have a choice. The winds of change were blowing through OA, clearing the air and bringing new ideas in their wake.

Chapter Twelve

More Food
for Thought

LOWN about by varying opinions, the carbohydrate controversy and food plans in general would continue to rage through every Conference for many years.

On the agenda sent out to delegates for our tenth annual National Conference in 1971, one of the items asked, "Should the O.A. National Service Office send out a selection of suggested guides for eating? If so, what eating plans should be suggested?"

A delegate from Fresno, California, opened the discussion with an impassioned plea for "guidelines from the central office" so the newcomers would know what to do. Other delegates agreed with him. Some even went so far as to say that they didn't care what eating plan was sent out. "Just give us guidelines so we know what to tell newcomers," they begged.

As national secretary, I gave the delegates a brief report on how we answered these pleas for help in the OA National Service Office. Then I went on to say, "This is the suggestion I have, and some of it can be lifted right out of *To The Newcomer* so that it wouldn't have to be Conference-approved again. [We could have] an umbrella introduction that talks about what is moderation, honesty in an eating plan, weighing and measuring your food, not skipping meals, and so forth."

"Now, we have a carbohydrate eating plan," I continued, "that has not been approved by any American Medical Association [AMA]. However, it is primarily just a list of low-carbohydrate foods and some portions to go by. There's only one thing missing, and that's the whole-grain category. This could be added and sent out, perhaps in an eating plan that *has* been approved by the AMA, as a suggested second plan, making that umbrella introduction as specific as possible.

"This is my suggestion: If we send out the carbohydrate [eating plan], which has been highly successful, and another kind with the same kinds of general suggestions about weighing and measuring that includes the whole grain categories of bread and cereal, we will at least offer a choice and a guideline without specifically endorsing an eating plan. . . ."

As each delegate responded, the general consensus appeared to be approval for my suggestion. Finally, the delegates authorized the National Service Office to publish the two eating plans with "an umbrella cover letter." I was elated at the vote, and the longer I thought about it, the more creative I became.

Not content with just a cover letter, I wrote an eight-page booklet, 8½-by-11 inches, on bright yellow paper. (All the better to catch a member's eye on the literature table!)

It was called "Suggested Guides for Abstaining from Compulsive Overeating." The first page read:

> On the following pages you will find five definitions and twelve suggested, specific guides to help you abstain from compulsive overeating. Many years of collective experience have proven these to be effective in helping to arrest our common illness, lose our excess weight, and maintain our normal weight.
>
> OVEREATERS ANONYMOUS DOES NOT ENDORSE ANY ONE SPECIFIC PLAN OF EATING. However, we realize that we must know what we <u>can</u> eat in order to know what we <u>cannot</u> eat. Therefore, in this booklet you will find two suggested eating plans, both based on three measured meals a day with nothing in between but low- or no-calorie beverages.
>
> There are no 'musts' in O.A. These eating plans are offered

as <u>suggestions only</u> to guide you on the physical level of this new way of living.

Before you choose either of these two plans, or any other, please consult your doctor. If you have any kind of medical problem which involves a different way of eating, please follow your doctor's prescribed plan. You will still be abstaining from compulsive overeating.

Remember—we eat because of what is eating us. Therefore, we must keep in mind that no eating plan, however good, will be permanently effective for us without the daily practice of the Twelve Steps on the spiritual and emotional levels as well.

Other pages of this booklet contained questions and answers about abstinence, eating plans, food sponsors and program sponsors. We also discussed weighing and measuring food, writing our plans, eating slowly while sitting down, calling before we took that first bite and other suggestions.

(For the first time, we emphasized a phrase which the "carbohydrate members" had been using for several years. "WHEN IN DOUBT, LEAVE IT OUT!" This statement is as valid for compulsive overeaters today as it was then, and we continued to use it as long as we printed food plans.)

The two center pages were the food plans. Pages 3 and 4 were called "Plan A—Low Carbohydrate (Suggested for losing weight)." They contained a sample daily menu and sixteen specific instructions on purchasing, preparing and eating allowed foods. They also gave a list of allowable foods and general suggestions for preparing them, along with a list of "foods we avoid."

Pages 5 and 6 introduced, for the first time in OA, "Plan B—Basic Four Food Groups (Suggested for losing weight)." Visually, pages 5 and 6 were set up the same as Plan A, but the information contained in them was different in several ways.

In 1970 I had met Marilyn Moore, a nutritionist in East Los Angeles who was a very supportive friend of OA. She believed in what we were doing and tried to spread our message in her daily work. Marilyn helped me to pull together Plan B.

I was concerned about the lack of Vitamin C, so we included "one citrus fruit." I also worried about the lack of calcium on Plan A, so we talked about "8 oz. skim milk daily." Then we brought in the foods I had always said were nutritionally vital to a balanced plan of eating—whole grain bread and a very small baked potato. We allowed lemon juice in tea between meals and limited milk or half-and-half in coffee. While we were at it, I asked Marilyn about a six-ounce can of tomato juice, because that's what I was taking whenever I had to carry my lunch with me. She said, "Sure, why not? Just mention that juice isn't as filling as bulky vegetables."

I had also compiled information from books by Adelle Davis, a nationally-known nutritionist, the American Medical Association and Weight Watchers.

Note that the only difference between Plans A and B was that Plan B included "one baked potato—very small, whole-grain bread—one slice, skim milk—one 8 oz. glass and tomato juice—6 oz."

In planning the layout for the booklet, I had a bright idea. "Let's print the two food plans on paper perforated along the inside fold. Then the member can tear out the preferred plan and carry it around." I was so proud of that brainstorm.

Much later, I discovered my idea had really backfired. When the Valley secretaries received their booklet orders, they simply tore out Plan B before their members could see it. Censorship had infiltrated our ranks, and we didn't even realize it.

Maxine, who was still OA's national treasurer, kept a watchful eye over the accuracy of the Plan A printing. We made a few minor changes to it. Maxine and the Van Nuys members gave their approval for this, happy that their plan would be printed by OA at last.

A draft of the new booklet went to the trustees. At the board meeting of September 18, 1971, the trustees approved the layout, made some changes in content and voted to proceed with our newest publication.

In 1964 John W. had joined the Van Nuys group, where

he became abstinent using the Gray Sheet. John was one of the first male members in the Valley, and when he moved to Orange County (south of Los Angeles) in 1965, he took with him the Van Nuys approach to the program. To remain abstinent, John started a group for low-carbohydrate abstainers in the city of Westminster, California. Like the Van Nuys group, the Westminster group had strict rules for working the program and for eating according to the Gray Sheet.

In the early 1970s several Orange County members, all carbohydrate abstainers, formed a special OA group called Las Flacas ("The Thin Ones") Maintainers Group. Still adamantly opposed to the vote of the 1971 Conference, they submitted a proposal for the 1972 Conference. They wanted OA to officially endorse the overeaters' allergy to refined sugar and flour. In addition, they asked the delegates to publish only Plan A and a new plan they had compiled for "maintaining abstinence." The delegates did not endorse the proposed allergy definition.

However, after long and heated discussions, the delegates finally agreed to publish three "disciplined" eating plans— "For losing weight, Plan A low-carbohydrate, or Plan B basic-four food groups. For maintaining normal weight, a low-carbohydrate maintenance plan."

A simple irony was lost on us. Although we had always insisted that OA was not a diet club, we spent at least half of that 1972 Conference discussing what foods should be included on the Gray Sheet and whether or not we could mix proteins. The motion to mix fruits was ruled out of order. Still, the delegates reaffirmed that even though these plans were being published by OA, "OA does not endorse any specific eating plan."

The prior year's large yellow pamphlet was discontinued. The two plans for losing weight were printed separately, Plan A on gray paper and Plan B on orange paper.

Food arguments continued during every Conference for the next five years. I vividly remember standing at the center microphone one year, waiting my turn to give some historical information. I was to be the last person to speak. Suddenly, without warning, a young girl ran up behind me and grabbed the microphone out of my hands. Voice shaking, she shouted, "I was sent by my New York intergroup to make sure we included an eighth of a cup of wheat germ on this food plan!"

Our annual Conference wasn't the only place for wholesale food fights. Sometime during the summer of 1972, the California Westminster philosophy took root in New York. Called "OA Westminster," it became a movement unto itself with rules and Gray Sheet abstinence requirements. (Other, more rigid offshoots would later be called "OA Plus" and "Cambridge.")

OA had begun in New York in the mid-1960s. By 1972, Gray Sheet was the food plan being zealously pitched in New York's OA meetings, as it was in many groups across the country in those years.

That summer a member of an OA group on Long Island in Levittown, New York went to a meeting in New York City at the Moravian Church at 30th Street and Lexington. That night she heard Arthur and Dorothy talk about the group in Westminster, California where people worked the program in a very structured, disciplined way. Their enthusiasm appealed to the Long Island member, and the next week she returned with others from her group, including Phyllis F. and Sam G.

Arthur and Dorothy had brought with them from California information which was expanded into a set of questions which were given to the Long Island members. Then Bobbie, Phyllis, Sam and others decided to start working the program as the original Westminster group did, with the addition of answering the questions in writing as part of their discipline.

Phyllis recalls some of the questions as being ". . . really dumb. I remember one was, 'What is the medulla oblongata?' But I was willing to go to any lengths. I answered those dumb questions, starting in July of 1972."

In September the three of them began a new OA group

in Amityville, New York, which they called the "Westminster" group.

When they started this new group, remembers Phyllis, "We decided the questions were too dumb, and we rewrote them." Sitting at the dining room table in Phyllis's home, four members of the Amityville group composed what came to be known in New York OA as the "Westminster Questions." These were twenty-one questions concerning Steps One, Two, and Three, which were to be answered in writing on twenty-one consecutive days. They were followed by nine questions about the OA tools which also had to be answered, one each day.

"There was no messing around," Phyllis reminisces. "You had to do an assignment every day. After thirty days you had a 'stepping-up' ceremony, and then you became a sponsor." The stepping-up ceremony was "almost like a religious ceremony" with a format of its own. "You read what you'd written on a certain one of the assignments, and you were given a little plant to mark the occasion."

According to Phyllis, "The Long Island Westminster program took off like a forest fire. In no time there were Westminster OA meetings every day and night."

The regular OA meetings in New York did not coexist easily with the Westminster forest fire, and soon the heat between them became almost unbearable. It was the same argument that had raged at the 1964 National Conference.

"They complained we were breaking the Traditions with our way of working the program," Phyllis reflects. "We felt we were strengthening OA. In our meetings I heard about the Twelve-Step program and how to abstain and recover instead of about how to accept slips. I didn't want to come to meetings and hear, 'I binged today, but it's okay. . . .'

"We believed we weren't breaking the Traditions because we didn't tell people they couldn't be in OA if they didn't want to work it the Westminster way. We told them this was what we did to recover. If they didn't want to do what we did, they could go to "regular OA" meetings. This is why meetings are autonomous, so we can have a choice about what kind of meetings we attend. In Westminster OA we had meetings where people were committed to working the Steps and using the tools in a structured, disciplined way. At the same time, we respected OA as a whole and wanted to be a part of it."

By 1975 the Westminster program had successfully grown large enough to have a separate intergroup. That year Phyllis and Sam were sent as delegates to the World Service Conference.

During the Conference, Phyllis was amazed at the hostility shown to them by some of the delegates. She remembers, "One woman came up to us and told us, 'You stand for everything I hate.'" Nevertheless, Sam was elected to the World Service Board of Trustees, one of the first trustees from New York.

In 1977, the delegates at the World Service Conference voted to adopt a new food plan, "Suggested Abstinence Guide for Losing Weight," replacing Plans A and B. Printed on blue paper, it became known as "Blue Sheet."

According to the flyer sent out from the World Service Office introducing the new plan, "This plan is nutritionally sound and should be used in conjunction with the O.A. pamphlet, *Good Nutrition—A Vital Ingredient of Abstinence.* Both of these pieces of literature were written with the help of medical authorities and nutritionists."

However, we simply couldn't let go of our anguish over eating plans in Overeaters Anonymous. Just one year later, at the end of the 1978 Conference, the delegates voted to publish a booklet of several nutritionally-sound food plans to replace the Blue Sheet approved in 1977. I was extremely upset at this vote, since I felt that OA should not endorse any food plans at all. Our recovery, I firmly believed, lay in the Twelve Steps and Twelve Traditions.

That booklet, which we called *The Dignity Of Choice*, contained not one or two, but *eight* different food plans! These were called "Basic Four," "Sugar and Flour-free,"

"Vegetarian," "Youth," "Medical," "Modified Carbohydrate," "No Refined Carbohydrates" and "Maintenance." As usual, we included lists of food under various categories. Slowly but surely we had been moving into the field of nutrition, despite our insistence that OA wasn't a diet club.

Dignity of Choice was published in early 1979 and sold at meetings until 1987, when the next major food-related event took place in OA.

During the twenty-sixth World Service Conference in 1987, after much debate and with input from our legal counsel, the delegates approved a policy statement which was to affect OA for many years. The statement read:

> The OA 1987 World Service Conference, after careful consideration, believes that offering food plans at OA meetings is a violation of Tradition Ten.
>
> While each individual OA member is free to choose their own personal plan for abstinence, OA as a whole cannot print, endorse or distribute food plan information to members.
>
> Nutrition is a most controversial outside issue; the hiring of professionals to produce food plans for use at meetings also violates the Eighth Tradition, as we need always remain non-professional. Groups endorsing any food plans by distributing them at their meetings affect OA as a whole.
>
> We ask all groups, intergroups and regions of OA to adhere to the above policy statement and discontinue the use of food plan information at meetings.
>
> We ought best concern ourselves with our suggested program of recovery—the Twelve Steps.

In the meantime, another low-carbohydrate obsession had taken hold in Phoenix, Arizona.

In 1985 several OA members, unhappy with what they called the "fat-serenity" groups in Phoenix, decided to form their own groups. Using the initials from AA's phrase—Honesty, Open-mindedness, Willingness—they called their groups OA-HOW.

Many of these members had belonged to the Westminster groups in New York. While they believed in the practice of the Twelve Steps and Twelve Traditions, they felt that just offering these principles wasn't enough. Overeaters needed discipline and structure, they urged, so they embraced many elements of the Westminster food plan, questions, sponsor guides and other practices and requirements they had followed earlier. Unfortunately, they also began going to existing OA groups in Phoenix, disrupting the meetings and speaking out against the way the program was being worked in what they called the "regular OA" groups.

Nineteen-eighty-five was a rerun of Irene's activities twenty years earlier. Only the faces had changed; the uproar was the same.

Then in 1995, in an action reminiscent of Irene's departure three decades earlier, one of the initiators of the HOW groups walked out of OA and started his own organization.

Meanwhile, I was beginning to understand that some overeaters need to be given guidelines in order to learn how to eat healthfully while they discover how to change their thinking and living.

Irene's sheets—gold, pink and green—OA's Gray and Blue Sheets and *Dignity of Choice*, Westminster, Cambridge, OA Plus and HOW; all of these were brave attempts to keep us focused as we trudged the road of happy destiny.

Nevertheless, I still believed that our basic, long-term recovery lay in the daily practice of the Twelve Steps and Twelve Traditions.

What could we do to end the incessant food fights and achieve loving unity among our members? Suddenly, the unexpected happened. During the 1995 World Service Conference, an important motion was brought to the floor:

> It is moved to replace "abstinence" as a tool with "a plan of eating," and to emphasize abstinence as outlined in the OA Preamble—"Our primary purpose is to abstain from compulsive overeating and to carry this message of recovery to those who still suffer."

Amidst great enthusiasm, an obvious majority of the delegates voted in favor of this motion. With that vote, we came full circle. Since 1962 I had insisted that the word "abstinence" meant the act of "staying away from." For many years I had said, "An eating plan is the means by which we nourish our bodies. That plan may be different for each of us, but 'staying away from compulsive overeating,' or 'abstaining,' is the same for every OA member." Now, the World Service delegates had formally recognized that distinction.

Looking back, we can see that our path to recovery has been scattered with both pitfalls and successes, but if we continue to work together in unity, we will fulfill the miraculous promise of the Twelve Steps.

After all, it was our similarities and not our differences that brought us into the healing rooms of Overeaters Anonymous. It will always be that common need that helps us fulfill our hearts' yearning—recovery from the bondage of compulsive overeating.

Chapter Thirteen

Weaving the Fabric of Our Lives

*T*HE development of Overeaters Anonymous has been similar to the creation of a beautiful tapestry. One thread will be woven in to form part of the pattern; soon another thread is introduced, then another. Eventually, a thread is temporarily dropped so that another can be brought in to enhance the total effect. Sometimes a mistake is made, and the weaving has to be redone to achieve the desired result.

So it has been with growth of OA. While the carbohydrate controversy seemed to totally consume our concentration, other pieces of the pattern were being developed as we went along. Together we were weaving the threads of the OA story into the fabric of our lives.

One of the earliest elements of this design was our General Service Office (GSO), established in my small dining room. Because I had difficulty in letting go and delegating tasks, I handled nearly everything during the first few years.

By early 1963, OA had grown so fast that the amount of work was overwhelming. I had no choice but to ask for help, and Rochelle P. came to the rescue by volunteering to answer many of the letters. Still, the workload increased.

Finally, I decided to give up managing our financial matters. Although OA still didn't have much money, it was just one more thing for me to do.

Maxine R. was an enthusiastic member who'd been with us since September, 1961, and she had lost considerable weight. Equally important to me, she had some knowledge of bookkeeping. We had a lot in common, since she was also a young wife with two little girls.

I had been friendly with Maxine before she moved from Los Angeles to the Valley in early 1963. There, as I described earlier, she not only became a carbohydrate-abstainer, but Irene became her sponsor. Nevertheless, I was desperate.

Putting my pride aside, I called her one night to ask if she would be OA's treasurer. After hearing what needed to be done, she agreed.

I was relieved and tremendously grateful. We made arrangements for me to bring the money and all the paperwork to her house one evening in March, 1963.

Years later, in 1989, I interviewed Maxine about her early OA participation. Laughing, she reminisced, "I remember you coming here, sitting at this kitchen table with a little black book. [It was] the little ledger that you brought, that you'd been keeping track of the money in, and if I'm not wrong, it was twenty-six dollars. It was some little infinitesimal amount of money."

"Tell me more," I prodded her.

Brow furrowed, she tried to recall the events. "Well," she said, "we had talked on the phone, and you had asked me if I would do the bookkeeping. I said I knew how to do bookkeeping.

"You said, 'Well, that part of it's getting a little bit too much for me. I have so many other things. . . .'

"You know," Maxine went on, "you were running everything else. In some respects, I guess you thought if you could get rid of that, or have somebody else do it. . . . I think that was probably the first time you were really ready to relinquish anything out of your control. And so you came here with the little book, and I think the checkbook. . . .

"And so I remember opening a checking account at Crocker [Bank] right here in Van Nuys and transferring all the money. I took over all the finances."

At the board meeting of May 12, 1963, Maxine was formally elected OA's first national treasurer. Since there was no money to pay her, Maxine donated her time, telling us it was a labor of love.

At OA's 30th birthday celebration in 1990, Maxine reminisced again. "As OA . . . started having Conventions [immediately following the annual Conference], money started to come in, and OA started to grow financially. I can remember that I used to handle *all* the money from *all* the Conventions. We didn't have registration like we have now. . . . we used to pass the basket at every single meeting. Every time there was a panel or speaker, we passed the basket. Needless to say, we had very large bags of change. After one of these Conference-Conventions, my husband would come (like all these faithful husbands, these wonderful, saintly men who stayed married to compulsive overeaters). He and I used to sit at my kitchen table and roll coins by hand, year after year."

However, during OA's fourth year, 1963, OA had just enough money for running expenses. The minutes of the second board meeting on October 27, 1962, read: "A motion was made and passed that a token salary of $25.00 per month be paid to Rozanne in payment for her duties as National Secretary of Overeaters Anonymous." That was OA's first application of Tradition Eight: "Overeaters Anonymous should remain forever nonprofessional, but our service centers may employ special workers."

Our income was still extremely small. One year later, the minutes of the board meeting of October 19, 1963, read: "By unanimous vote, the Board decided that no additional salaries be paid at this time."

As our workload increased, our volunteers' enthusiasm decreased rapidly. A letter I wrote to A.G. on March 19, 1964, describes the situation:

> I'm enclosing [a letter] to you from up north. Believe me, the day I got that letter, I felt like throwing the whole office, typewriter and all, right in the face of all OA. Unfortunately, just the day before, Rochelle had informed me that she could no longer help in the office or mail out literature, and I felt as though the walls were closing in on me. At that point Debbie, my seven-year-old, volunteered to help me after dinner every

night, which I thought was very touching. One of the local members said she'd take the literature order-mailing until the end of June, but so far we haven't been able to get any other volunteers. I could use someone else to help answer letters, too. I don't even get my own family's mending done, and I just manage to stay even on laundry and cleaning. However . . . I have calmed down . . . and have really asked God for help and left it up to Him.

As usual, my solution was just around the corner. The local member mentioned in my letter to A.G. was Hilda N., and her short-term offer eventually stretched out nine years.

Meanwhile, my dining room held the correspondence files. Many nights I worked until midnight or beyond, answering letters from groups, replying to inquiries, writing long three- or four-page letters to overexcited members of new groups with growing pains and problems.

Just as I reached my limit, Margaret P. appeared on the scene. She had come to OA in 1963, began abstaining from her very first meeting and lost considerable weight. Margaret had been an executive secretary and knew how to run both an office and a business.

In the summer of 1964, Margaret asked me if she could help with office work and correspondence. I welcomed her eagerly; finally, I had a teammate in the office.

Now we had four women supporting our little General Service Office. Maxine, Hilda and Margaret were all volunteers putting in many love-filled hours of work. I was still office director at a salary of twenty-five dollars a month. I picked up the mail at our post office box, distributed the contents to the proper person and answered the mail with Margaret's assistance.

In addition, Esther G. had begun to help Hilda. Both women had come into OA in 1961. A tall, statuesque woman, Esther had lost seventy-five pounds and wanted to return the blessings she had received. Hilda was short and plump, and her cheery disposition made everyone feel wonderful. The two women lived within a block of one another, and since Hilda didn't drive, Esther took her to every available OA meeting. Their friendship was to play a vital role in the future of our growing General Service Office.

That ever-increasing GSO workload was reflected in the board meeting minutes of October 24, 1964: "Gene S. made a motion that the salary of the National Secretary be raised from $25.00 to $50.00 per month. Norma B. seconded the motion, and it was approved by the Board unanimously." During that same meeting, the board also voted to buy a new typewriter and table for the office. For the first time, we would have equipment of our own.

Two months later, on December 14, 1965, A.G. resigned from the Board of Trustees. That was a tremendous blow to me; I felt I had lost a dear friend and a supportive advisor. However, my home and OA office life were so hectic, I barely had time to grieve over the situation.

Thankfully, Margaret continued to answer many of the letters. Since those were the days before photocopying machines and computers, she typed the stencils at her husband's office and ran off meeting directories, formats, and anything else we might need in quantity. Maxine was taking care of OA's finances, keeping the books and records of contributions and expenses.

Hilda had taken some of the literature into her home, but I was still trying to manage everything. For months Hilda had pleaded, "Rozanne, let me take all the literature. The printer can deliver all the pamphlets and order forms to me, and I can fill the orders and take that burden off your shoulders." Finally, I gave in.

In January, 1965, we moved all the boxes and cartons of literature and order forms into Hilda's spare room. That room (and later her garage) became OA's first literature warehouse. That move was not a moment too soon!

A few weeks earlier a grateful OA member had written to Dear Abby. This is a portion of her letter, which appeared in Abby's column on February 25, 1965.

Dear Abby,

In answer to Fat and Disgusted's cry for help. . . . I have [a] suggestion. It's a club called "Overeaters Anonymous."

Please don't laugh. Compulsive eaters suffer from the same type of illness that compulsive drinkers suffer from, and OA has the solution to this problem. I know because it worked for me and for many of my friends. We help each other, just as alcoholics who belong to AA help each other. If anyone wishes more information about our group, the address is P.O. Box 3372, Beverly Hills. Thank you. We are anonymous, so just sign me—BACK TO NORMAL

Since our grateful member had neglected to forewarn me about that letter, I was totally unprepared for the results.

Blissfully ignorant, one February morning I made my daily trip into our Beverly Hills post office box to pick up the mail. We'd been receiving twenty-five to thirty letters a week, but suddenly, that was about to change. Opening the little door, I could see just a couple of letters and a yellow notice asking me to see the postmaster.

I went over to the counter. "Is there a problem?" I asked the man in charge. He just laughed and nodded his head, motioning me to follow him into another room. He opened the door and showed me sacks and sacks of mail. I assumed it was a postal storage room. Oh, was I wrong!

"What kind of business are you running?" he demanded. "This is just a small, neighborhood post office. We're not set up for this kind of influx."

"Is this *all* for Overeaters Anonymous?" I was incredulous. "We are a very small organization," I apologized. "I have no idea what this is all about." Then I asked to see a few of the letters. As I began reading, I was stunned. I showed the postmaster what had come in the mail. These were obviously responses to the letter in Dear Abby's column. We both knew more would be coming. He was very kind and assured me the personnel would work with me.

I lugged those mail sacks out to the car, wondering how we were going to handle what lay ahead. Those letters were only a ripple; the tidal waves washed in over the

next few months. The final count was seven thousand letters.

As soon as I arrived home, I frantically called Margaret
and Hilda. "Calm down," they both reassured me. "Everything will be taken care of, one day at a time."

"Debbie and Julie will be home from school soon," I
pleaded to Margaret. "What should I do first?"

"I'm on my way over," Margaret said. "Put a load of laundry in the washer and sit tight. We'll figure it out."

Margaret lived just a few blocks from me, and she was at
my house in five minutes. Together we started opening the
letters. Some of the letters contained donations of money,
some just wanted information, others were heart-rending
pleas for help. More mail arrived each day.

I remember one Monday morning. With sacks filled with
twenty-five-hundred letters stacked at the back of my
kitchen, I couldn't even get into the laundry alcove to do the
weekly wash.

That day I took Debbie and Julie with me to the post office. As I struggled out with more mail packs slung across my
back, Debbie piped up, "Mommy, you look just like Santa
Claus."

Margaret and I met to discuss how best to handle the situation. Remembering our experience after the Paul Coates
telecast, I knew our first answer had to be a form letter, with
a tear-off portion on the bottom just like the one we'd used
four years earlier. I was very proud of this new "Miracle
Letter," and we continued to use it for many other publicity
responses through the next six years.

Here's the first reply we sent to those seven thousand
people who wrote to us after the Dear Abby article in early
1965:

HOW MIRACLES <u>CAN</u> HAPPEN!

This is an open letter to all of you who have written to us
asking about Overeaters Anonymous. We are grateful for your
interest, and want to share with you the hope, strength and
encouragement that has come to us through the wonderful
OA program of recovery.

In the past, all of us in OA had tried many methods of weight reduction and control. Diet doctors, shots, pills, psychiatry, hypnosis, fad diets, rest farms . . . all of these are fine in their respective places, but for most compulsive overeaters like us they had only been temporary solutions. Many of us would indeed lose weight, only to gain back more than ever before. You see, we thought that food alone was our problem. What we didn't know was that it was the feelings which lay behind our overeating which were causing all the trouble.

How many times we had heard it said, "If you'd only use a little will power, you could lose all that weight." Or, "You have such a pretty face, dear, if only you weren't so heavy." And particularly for the men, "Don't you know you're asking for a heart attack with all that extra poundage?" Many times we'd eat out of frustration, resentment or self-pity, only to wake up the next morning saying, "Today's the day I'll start my diet, and I'll never go off again!" Of course, our good resolutions never lasted very long, and we were soon back on the same old merry-go-round of diets and binges.

These things have been common to all of us in OA, but now, for the first time in our lives, we all have HOPE! We find that within the fellowship of Overeaters Anonymous we are not alone. We meet others who have suffered as we have, and they offer us love, compassion and complete understanding of our common problem. In OA we can bring our feelings out into the open. Here we find willing ears and sympathetic hearts; people who are not judging us for our actions and who are ready to share their strength as we make the long journey back to recovery. We discover that we help ourselves most by helping others with the same problem. We learn that we must honestly admit to our innermost selves that we are compulsive overeaters and are powerless over food. This is the first step toward recovery.

Overeaters Anonymous has given us what we have never had before . . . a proven, workable method by which we have been able to arrest our common illness, one day at a time! The OA recovery program is identical with that of Alcoholics Anonymous; we use the same Twelve Steps and Twelve Traditions, changing only the words alcohol and alcoholic to food and compulsive overeater.

There are no dues or fees in order to join OA, (we are self-supporting through our own contributions). The only requirement for membership is a desire to stop eating compulsively.

To help you understand more about how OA works, we are enclosing a little pamphlet which will answer some of your questions; we're also sending a price list of our literature and our current Directory of meeting places.

Would you like to become part of the fellowship of Overeaters Anonymous? There are others from your area who have written us asking for help, and we would like to bring you together. It only takes two to make an OA group; and just think . . . you wouldn't be alone with your problem anymore!

Ever since our first meeting in January, 1960, we have found that OA has a workable program which is proving itself more and more successful every day. It is a miracle to those of us who had no hope . . . a gradual, steady proof of the fact that compulsive overeaters can share their problems and help each other to the benefit of themselves, their families, and the communities in which they live. In all humility, we hope you will help us by letting us help you.

Remember, if no one in your area wants to join in starting an OA group, then there is no way we can help you. Someone (or perhaps more than one) has to start the ball rolling where there are no existing OA groups. Don't be afraid . . . we will do everything we can to support and encourage you in your efforts! Please send 25 cents for postage and handling. Return to: Overeaters Anonymous, P.O. Box 3372, Beverly Hills, California 90212.

☐　I wish to join an OA group. You have my permission to send my name and address to my nearest group starter or starters.

☐　I am desperate! If no one in my area wants to start a group, then send me their names (you can give them mine, too), and we'll all try to start an OA group together.

Name _____

Address _____

City _____State _____

Phone number_____ Zip Code _____

During those first couple of weeks I would bring the mail home. Then Margaret and I would sort the letters, sending money to Maxine and literature orders to Hilda. Many letters we answered ourselves. Records were kept of every letter, every dime and dollar received. Finally, it was too much for the two of us.

Something had to be done immediately. My home and my life had been turned upside down. Even my patient Marvin was beginning to comment.

That's when Hilda came to the rescue. At that time she lived alone, earning her living as a dressmaker. She volunteered her house to receive the mail after I picked it up in Beverly Hills. Esther went to the post office as well, delivering hundreds of letters to Hilda each day.

Hilda had a marvelously cheerful voice. During the years when she had the OA phone in her home, I used to call her "OA's voice of sunshine."

When I interviewed Hilda in 1982, she remembered: "My living room, honey, was filled halfway up to the ceiling with the cartons. For ten years I could not serve my family because the cartons held up the dining room table. But I thought I wasn't doing anything special. I was so glad it was me doing it, that was all."

"How did we handle it [the response]?" I asked her.

"I set up crews," she answered. "They would leave the house at maybe eleven o'clock at night. I'd work 'til two o'clock in the morning, [then] have the dining room table cleared off."

"Who were these crews?" I prodded her.

She thought for a moment, then grinned. "Honey, they came from all over. . . . I'm talking about only OA members. . . . They came six and eight and ten at a time, every day . . . they were marvelous. . . . They stuffed, and they also wrote envelopes." I remembered that several of the husbands also volunteered during that period.

"And they helped sort?" I asked.

"Well, Esther and I did the sorting," she answered. "We had separated the batches. . . . Whenever we separated anything that felt like money, Esther took care of that . . . right away. A lot [of letter writers] sent donations. The rest of us . . . separated them into categories. Some wanted only information. Some had to be handled specially; that went to Margaret. . . . she had a gift for writing. Other than that, we would separate by cities. If it was local, we separated by zones. All that I did when everybody left. I think that's how I lost my weight," she laughed, "'cause I didn't have time to eat."

During that period I was completely overwhelmed. Eventually, the chaos caught up with me, and on May 21, 1965, I resigned as national secretary. Two days later, Margaret was selected by the trustees to take my place.

An interesting paragraph from the board meeting minutes of May 23, 1965, shows our second application of Tradition Six:

> Discussion of salaries for General Service Office workers was begun with the salary for treasurer. Number of hours spent and degree of responsibility were mentioned. . . . The question was, can we afford it? It was brought out that most delegates felt since the groups would now be aware that more money was needed . . . more would be coming in. It was decided that in order to expand, we must begin to pay our service center workers.

The result was that Margaret, our national secretary, would receive fifty dollars per month and Maxine, our national treasurer, would receive twenty dollars per month. In addition, the two GSO assistants, Hilda and Esther, would be paid fifteen dollars a month each. This was a big step forward for OA—our first paid office staff!

The meeting minutes went on:

> The [salary] schedule was approved with the agreement that if enough money did not come in, the salaries would cease for awhile.

The OA phone was moved from my dining room to Hilda's home, and the new number was to be listed in the Los Angeles central telephone directory. As always, Maxine was very concerned "for all the money we were spending that we didn't have." Despite her protestations, the trustees voted to buy a new electric typewriter and file cabinet for Margaret.

For the next six years, our General Service Office would be located in the homes of four devoted members. These women were described in *I Put My Hand In Yours*, written in 1968 (paraphrased here):

> Margaret P.—National Secretary. She maintains contacts with all O.A. groups and "loners." She also corresponds with various outside agencies who inquire about O.A., and she keeps the Directory of Meeting Places up to date. Margaret coordinates and plans O.A.'s annual National Conference.

(During OA's early years, there were no Conference trustees or committees. With input only from the trustees, I had put on our first four Conferences by myself. Margaret carried out the next five Conferences in the same manner.)

> Hilda N.—She maintains the O.A. main office in her home. The O.A. telephone is there, and Hilda is on call twenty-four hours a day. She fills all literature orders (on the day of receipt or the very next day!), wraps and packs all bulk mail and sends out starter kits to new O.A. groups.
>
> Esther G.—She picks up all incoming mail at the Beverly Hills P.O. Box and sorts it for distribution to the Treasurer, Lifeline Editor, literature office and the National Secretary. After double-checking all literature orders, she takes them to the post office for mailing. Esther is also the telephone liaison between G.S.O. and the various groups.
>
> Maxine R.—O.A. Treasurer. She handles every bit of money coming into the O.A. office makes payments keeps O.A. money affairs in order and up to date. She works with the accountant, and compiles the annual financial report presented each year at our National Conference.
>
> Rozanne S.—She acts in an advisory capacity to the National Secretary, Lifeline Editor, O.A. Trustees and the General Service Office. Since the beginning of O.A., she has been responsible for the development, writing and production of the O.A. literature.

GSO was renamed National Service Office in 1970. Then, unexpectedly, tragedy struck. Margaret fell desperately ill with lung cancer, and on May 9, 1971, we lost our beloved and loyal friend.

When Margaret entered the hospital, the annual Conference was only four months off, and Esther called me in a panic. "Rozanne," she wailed, "the Conference is coming, and I don't know what to do."

"Never mind, Esther," I consoled her, "I'll come back to the office to help until we get someone else."

(In May, 1969, salaries had been increased to fifty dollars per month each for Margaret, Hilda and Esther, and twenty-five dollars per month for Maxine. The following year all salaries were raised to seventy-five dollars per month, and in February, 1971, Hilda and Esther were each given one hundred dollars a month.)

When I took over Margaret's duties, it was clear that we were bursting at our office seams. When I resigned as national secretary in April, 1972, the trustees began a series of discussions about moving the office out of our homes and into an office. They also embarked on a search for a secretary and a location. On July 28, 1972, Pat C. was hired as World Service secretary for $375 per month plus $25 car allowance. She was expected to work full time, doing all the work that Hilda, Esther and Margaret had done. It was a big order.

On October 24, 1972, the board voted to share an office in a small commercial building in West Los Angeles with Southern California Central Service (forerunner of Los Angeles Intergroup). A year earlier, on November 20, 1971, the trustees had approved a change in our office name to World Service Office. Now, in late 1972, there was a widespread feeling that "we're no longer a 'mom-and-pop' operation; now we have a 'real' office and secretary."

After that, our World Service Office grew rapidly. By autumn of 1973 the trustees began searching for someone to provide professional business counseling. On September 25, 1973, Ralph McIntire, a non-OA independent management consultant, was approved by the board. Delighted by the prospect of his skills and expertise, we privately called him our "efficiency expert."

Pat was still trying to do the work of three people. When I interviewed Ralph in 1988, he recalled, "The trustees were trying to figure out how they could organize the work so Pat could do it all, which was simply an impossibility. My task was to work out a breakdown of the duties to figure out what Pat could do and what they needed somebody else to do. I spent a month at the office and gave the trustees my report, outlining a new way to operate."

The following year we moved into our own office in West Los Angeles. It was a small home which had been rezoned for commercial use. Pat continued as WSO secretary, and to ease her workload, non-OA Toni Berg was hired as office manager.

According to the board meeting minutes of November 5, 1974:

> The Board agrees that it establish a policy that you get what you pay for. That volunteers were not the way to run a business and that at present we discontinue all volunteer help in the office.

The next month Peter B. was hired as executive director at $1,000 per month. Pat remained as WSO secretary until her resignation in February, 1975. Her job, she said, had become increasingly time-consuming, overwhelming her family responsibilities.

The office continued to grow. Early in 1976 Maxine resigned as OA's national treasurer, after fourteen years of dedicated, hardworking service to Overeaters Anonymous.

In the fall of 1976, the World Service Office moved out of its little office and into a full-scale business operation in Torrance, thirty minutes south of West Los Angeles.

Two years after that, Peter resigned. The trustees asked Dr. Ralph McIntire (our 1973 business consultant) to serve freelance as the WSO general manager for six months, then for another six months.

Years later, Ralph reflected, "At the end of the second six

months, I told the Board of Trustees, 'You know, this is ridiculous. I've been here for a whole year now, and if you haven't found anybody, why don't you just put me on the payroll?'"

Although the trustees were hesitant about having a non-member run the office, they took a collective deep breath and hired Ralph as executive director in September, 1978.

For the next ten years Ralph guided OA's World Service Office affairs, transforming us from a struggling, inefficient operation into a businesslike, financially-sound corporation.

Ralph had decided that he would retire in September, 1988. In anticipation of this change, on August 17, 1988, the Board of Trustees hired another non-OA, Jorge Sever, as our new executive director.

Under Jorge's capable management, we moved twice more in the Torrance area, each time to larger quarters.

For thirty-five years our main OA office wandered throughout the Los Angeles area in search of a suitable home. From my dining room to two small commercial spaces in West Los Angeles to three larger places in nearby Torrance, nothing seemed to keep pace with our growing needs.

In addition, our decreased income due to the slowdown of local and national economies necessitated a major change for Overeaters Anonymous World Service Office.

Following an appropriate business relocation study, the Board of Trustees decided to move the office to Rio Rancho, just outside of Albuquerque, New Mexico.

After spending our formative years in the comfort and close proximity of our nurtured beginnings, we ventured forth to a different environment.

The opening ceremony for our beautiful new building was held in Rio Rancho on November 11, 1994. It was another thread in the magnificent fabric we were weaving for OA, for ourselves, and for all the compulsive overeaters who would come to us in the years ahead.

Chapter Fourteen

The Story of the OA Logo

I N looking back, another element of the OA pattern appeared on the surface of my memories.

It was autumn of 1969, and OA's tenth birthday was fast approaching. "How exciting!' we exclaimed to one another. "What can we do to celebrate this momentous occasion?"

All that year Margaret, our national secretary, had been exploring several new options. Periodically she would say to me, "Rozanne, OA needs a logo, a visual representation of our Fellowship. Other organizations have logos, why shouldn't we? It would be a great way to mark our first decade." We both agreed that it was terrific idea, but for a long time nothing came of our discussions.

Then, in the minutes of the OA Board of Trustees meeting on February 7, 1970, the first recorded mention of this idea appears:

> Margaret presented a handsome logo, made by her husband, to represent OA. . . .

I can still hear the gasp of surprise at that meeting. We were all seated at a rectangular table—Chairperson Maxine, the trustees, Margaret and me. Margaret had just given her national secretary's report. Then she grinned and said, "I have one more item to present that wasn't on the agenda." Holding an outsize manila envelope, she slowly pulled out a large posterboard and held it up. "I've felt for some time that OA needed a logo," she said, "and my dear husband has designed and contributed this to us." With that, she showed us a professional ink rendition of our first visual symbol:

We were overwhelmed! No one had discussed this before at the trustees' meetings, but it was an idea whose time had come. After the excitement had died down, we held a short discussion. Then Shirley D. said, "I make a motion that a request be made through the *Lifeline* for contributions from members for other ideas." The motion was seconded and passed, and Maxine was put in charge of the project.

In keeping with the trustees' vote, the May, 1970, *Lifeline* ran a plea for a new logo. Here is the item, just as it was published:

> Okay, what's a logo? A LOGO is a combining form meaning a word, a speech or a discourse as in logogram which is a letter, a character or a symbol used to represent an entire word. e.g. $ for a dollar. Overeaters Anonymous needs a LOGO, so now that you know what it is, how about designing us one. Please send your LOGO for the consideration of the Board of Trustees . . . no later than June 1, 1970.

We all sat back to wait for the flood of entries. We waited, and we waited; then we waited some more. Nothing happened. Finally, we decided to consider Margaret's design. The minutes of the October 3, 1970, trustees' meeting state:

> Maxine presented a logo for OA to be submitted for approval. Motion . . . that all expenses to adopt logo and [to] copyright same be paid by general funds.

On November 30, 1970, Margaret wrote a letter to American Optical which said in part:

> It is our understanding that you have a well-known mark,

AO. We do not feel, however, that our logo would be a confusing similarity and our trademark attorney does not either. We want to be sure that you agree with our opinion. May we have your permission to use our logo for Overeaters Anonymous?

The minutes of the next trustees' meeting on December 5, 1970, show that progress was being made:

Maxine read a letter from Alan Shapiro, the attorney who is handling the OA logo. He did a federal search and found no other OA trademark, but did find a company (American Optical) with a similar trademark. He suggested writing a letter asking American Optical for permission to use the logo. Margaret has written the letter. If permission is denied, OA will have to find another kind of logo.

A single sentence in the minutes of the February 20, 1971 trustees' meeting reads: "Maxine will check on the status of the logo." Since American Optical hadn't responded to our letter by the end of April, we decided to use Margaret's design.

Three months later, the front of the envelope containing the delegates' packet carried five lines: "OVEREATERS ANONYMOUS 1OTH ANNUAL CONFERENCE, May 21-23, 1971, International Hotel, Los Angeles." Above these words was our brand-new logo, displayed in all its glory. The delegates loved it, and we all found it a source of pride for our Fellowship.

Soon it appeared on OA stationery, memo pads, literature and various WSO publications. From March, 1973, through October, 1976, a beautiful, full-page version was used on the first page of every issue of the *OA Lifeline*. In April, 1973, the trustees decided to use our logo and the Serenity Prayer as a fundraising effort on pens, key tags and stationery to be sold at the 1973 World Service Convention.

By 1975 events were getting out of hand. Individuals and intergroups in various areas of the United States were using the OA logo in manufacturing and selling pins, tie tacks, bracelets, rings in gold and silver as well as other items. On August 16, 1975, the trustees moved to inform groups that "according to Tradition Six, the Board neither supports nor endorses any outside enterprise."

As a result of all the commercial activity, on October 19, 1975, the trustees voted,

> . . . that as our lawyer suggested, the OA logo and name be copyrighted, as well as any of our literature which is not already copyrighted."

Time passed, and we believed American Optical had forgotten about us. Unexpectedly, in late 1976 we received a letter from them objecting to OA's logo. Although there's no record in our OA files, their letter was probably triggered by our copyright application. (Peter B., our Executive Director, made a report at the trustees' meeting on August 22, 1976. "We hope," he said, "to work this out through personal contact with them.")

However, the two trademarks were admittedly similar, and the company continued to refuse permission. Finally, they issued us a deadline of January 18, 1978. After much worried discussion, at the March 5, 1977 trustees' meeting, Bill B. moved that we adopt a new "trademarkable" logo. The motion passed, and the search was on for a professionally-produced design. Once more it was contest time!

The March/April, 1978, *WSO Notebook* reported the search results:

> While it is not possible to acknowledge each entry submitted in our logo contest, WSO joins the board in extending special thanks to all OA members who sent in their work. Each design was carefully considered, and many were selected for final judging.
>
> For a number of reasons, however, it proved impossible to make a final choice. The most popular designs were found to belong to various companies and organizations, and a few of the best entries were even seen on the sides of trucks and displayed on billboards.

It became evident that we needed professional help. We turned to Art S., a longtime OA member, whose company had been printing our literature for several years. With his guidance and the board's approval, the creative challenge was given to Robert Boden, a professional graphic designer. Thanks to Art's capable supervision, Mr. Boden grasped our visual requirements and met our January deadline. On January 28, 1978, the trustees unanimously adopted the new design, and the delegates added their approval the following May. Our new logo was very different from the one we'd been using. The interesting rectangular pattern plus the words "Overeaters Anonymous" formed the total trademark:

OVEREATERS ANONYMOUS.®

It was a contemporary symbol to represent our fast-growing Fellowship. The March/April, 1978, *WSO Notebook* gives this artistic description:

> The letters "O" and "A" are rendered in abstract letterform. The centrally positioned "O" overlaps the "A" which is formed by the second and third portions of the three background sections of the symbol.
>
> These three sections represent the three aspects of the program of Overeaters Anonymous: physical, emotional and spiritual (the latter is represented by the lighter-toned left-hand portion).
>
> The two parallel diagonal lines have two distinct symbolic interpretations in addition to their basic function of delineating the letter "A":
>
> 1. The diagonals form a triangle at each end of the trademark; thus, the symbol for Alcoholics Anonymous is contained within the OA logo, as AA's principles are incorporated within the OA program.
>
> 2. The diagonal lines slashing through the design represent the internationally recognized symbol for abstinence, or desisting.

Our new design made its official debut on the cover of the April, 1978, *OA Lifeline*. Emblazoned in shades of bright and pale pink, it was an original and dramatic realization of Margaret's dream—a unique logo for Overeaters Anonymous.

Chapter Fifteen

The
OA Lifeline

*T*HE pattern of OA had begun to emerge during the months after the Paul Coates show. Many hands and minds were at work creating a new way of life for compulsive overeaters. Sometimes we made mistakes; sometimes we did everything right. Always we were trying to weave our differences into a unified whole.

Our first meeting directory on July 29, 1961, listed ten OA groups. Six months later we had added one more, and by the middle of 1962, OA had eighteen groups, including one in Chicago, Illinois.

As the lone worker in our first little office, I spent many hours answering inquiries about OA and writing very long letters to members of new groups with growing pains and questions.

By early 1962 it had become apparent to me that all these little groups needed to get together, to air their differences and unify their similarities. Our first effort was the Los Angeles area meeting described in Chapter Four.

However, there were only a few of us at the meeting that night. What about the rest of the OA members? I had an idea, one which I'd been considering for several months. "How about a conference of all the OA groups?" I asked them. "We could send out a letter inviting them to send a representative from each of our sixteen groups."

After compromising on our thornier issues that night, the

eight other Los Angeles women present welcomed this new idea. They asked me to write a letter to every group secretary and leader, proposing the conference and asking for input.

That letter turned out to be our first *Overeaters Anonymous Bulletin* (#1), dated May, 1962. (You'll find this three-page letter described in detail in Chapters Four and Eleven.)

It was followed in July by *Overeaters Anonymous Conference Bulletin #2*.

In September, shortly after the Conference, a third communication was mailed to the groups. It began, "TO ALL OA MEMBERS" and gave a detailed report on the results of the Conference votes as well as a plea for meeting directory updates. A.G.'s story was also included.

At the board meeting of February 9, 1963, A.G. brought up the idea of having a bimonthly *Bulletin*. His suggestion met with unanimous, enthusiastic approval, and Carol G. volunteered to take care of everything.

When she was unable to continue, a *Bulletin* committee was formed, consisting of Ethel K., Peggy S., June K. and Lorraine Z. By spring of 1963 I had been subscribing to the *AA Grapevine* for several months, and I was very impressed by the substance and format of this little magazine.

One night I brought the *Grapevine* to an *OA Bulletin* committee meeting. "We need something like this for OA," I said to the women. After much discussion, they agreed.

At our second National Conference, held in May, 1963, the idea of the proposed new magazine was enthusiastically received.

By late summer, our publication attempts finally succeeded in producing a new twenty-four page, 7-by-8½-inch magazine. It was called the *OA Bulletin*, Vol. I, Issue 1. The inside front cover stated: "This is the first issue of the *OA Bulletin*. It will be published bimonthly by Overeaters Anonymous. Subscription rates are $1.50 per year for six issues. Individual copies may be ordered for thirty-five cents per copy. For subscription blanks, please refer to back cover." It gave the address for the hoped-for submissions from members.

Much of the statement on the first page could have come from the pages of today's *OA Lifeline*. It read:

> This Bulletin represents the decision of Overeaters Anonymous to make available to all its members a bimonthly sharing place for O.A. ideas and news.
>
> It is hoped that the Bulletin will come to be a forum for the thoughts, feelings and growth of the individual O.A. member. It will inform its readership of the actions of the Board of Trustees and the results of the Annual Delegates' Conferences. Part of its purpose will be to attempt to minimize the geographical handicaps to communication between groups.
>
> It is the pledge of this magazine that, like O.A., it will grow and respond to the needs and desires of its participants. With the help of its readers it can come to represent the O.A. way of life as it is offered in the Twelve Steps and Twelve Traditions, and serve as a supporting companion in our daily lives. . . . We invite you to join with us in the creation of our O.A. Bulletin.

The next thirteen pages presented the "Report of [the] Second Annual Conference of Overeaters Anonymous, May 11, 1963, Los Angeles, California."

We listed the names and groups of the forty-eight delegates, the Board of Trustees and Maxine R., national treasurer. Following this was the first appearance of the newly-adopted "Guidelines of the National Conference of Overeaters Anonymous."

The next three pages printed inspiring quotes from ancient texts, a poem and the Serenity Prayer.

We finished with a pledge for future issues, a plea for submissions, a subscription blank and information on prices and publication dates.

The members' response to our first little magazine was very enthusiastic. By December, 1963, the second issue was ready to mail. It contained a letter from A.G. and five pages entitled "Overeaters Anonymous—How it Got Started," which told OA's history from the beginning through the Paul Coates TV telecast.

Following that was an important new OA subject, "The

Guidelines of the Northern California Regional Council Of Overeaters Anonymous." This was the first time that a local area had organized itself, and these Guidelines included groups from Fairfax, Inverness and San Rafael.

The last pages contained letters to the editor, more quotes from ancient and modern sources, a literature order list and subscription information and prices.

The *OA Bulletin* committee published one more issue in April, 1964, before the volunteers resigned. This issue included an announcement of the third annual Conference/Convention and the OA history through February, 1962.

During the May, 1964, Conference, Sue from Northern California volunteered to be the *OA Bulletin* editor. She assured the trustees that she'd appointed a committee and was ready to produce. True to her word, she published a *Bulletin* in August, 1964.

This issue contained abbreviated minutes of both the Third National OA Conference and the trustees' meeting of May 3, 1964. There were also letters to the editor, poems, group news and the usual literature and subscription information.

Alas, Sue's enthusiasm was short-lived, and we soon found ourselves without a publication or volunteer committee—again!

The problem was discussed at the October, 1964, board meeting. The minutes of that meeting read:

> It was agreed by the Board that the OA Bulletin material and funds be sent back to the GSO from Northern California. This will be held at GSO temporarily until we may determine who will be able and want to create another Bulletin editorial staff.
>
> The national secretary will write and send, upon approval of the Board of Trustees, a letter to each OA group explaining the problems of the Bulletin and ask for solutions and suggestions from each group. It will also be listed that temporarily we send no monies for future subscriptions. It was also suggested that the OA Bulletin be sold and handled as we have done with the printed literature . . . on a cash and carry basis.

It was suggested that the OA Bulletin list the functions and duties of the General Service Office as information of general interest to all OA members.

I was saddened by the situation. Each month the *AA Grapevine* appeared in my mailbox, and each month I became increasingly convinced that we needed something similar for our own Fellowship.

"Furthermore," I said to myself, "the name '*Bulletin*' just won't do. What can we have that's appealing and appropriate?" No matter how many options I considered, nothing seemed quite right.

Lying in bed late one night, I was thinking about this matter again. Unexpectedly, I had a mental image of a large ocean liner sailing near a helplessly bobbing lifeboat. Suddenly, someone from the liner tossed a strong rope to the little vessel.

"That's it," I exclaimed to myself, "a lifeline! What a perfect name for our magazine—*The OA Lifeline*."

The next day I made an excited call to Margaret, who was then our national secretary in the General Service Office. After describing what had happened the night before, I asked, "What do you think, Margaret?" "Oh, Rozanne," she answered, "what a great idea. You've hit on just the right title. That's exactly what this magazine will be, a lifeline between the members."

The board's response was equally enthusiastic. However, our immediate task was to find an editor for our newly-named publication.

Margaret mailed out a form to all group secretaries. It said:

THE OA LIFELINE NEEDS AN EDITOR! We are looking for an Editor for the OA Lifeline. The Editor will be paid. If you feel you are qualified for this exciting work, please fill out the form below and mail to: Margaret, P.O. Box 3372, Beverly Hills, California, 90212. Please answer promptly. Let's get our LIFELINE going again!

There was also space for describing background qualifications and OA membership information.

Wendy Z., a Los Angeles member, responded eagerly. She was warmly welcomed at the Fourth National Conference in May, 1965, and at the board meeting which followed.

The first issue of the *OA Lifeline*, Volume I, No. 1, was published in October, 1965. The redesigned format was a triumph, and OA members responded by subscribing in increasing numbers.

In addition to reports from our new editor, Wendy, and our new GSO secretary, Margaret, there were stories of recovery, poems, groups news, a pen-pal section and an update on the growth of OA. We now had eighty-nine groups, with more starting every month. Wendy also included reports on the Fourth National Conference and trustees' meeting in May, 1965.

For the next four years Wendy was a caring and talented editor for the *OA Lifeline*. As the Fellowship grew, the subscriptions increased, and *Lifeline* became part of our OA lives.

In late 1969, Wendy resigned as editor. She left a void that we tried to fill for the next seven years. Patty T., Nancy C., Teresa and Cynthia L. were OA members who served as editors, one after the other, to produce a magazine for the Fellowship. (Nancy and Cynthia each received fifty dollars an issue.) These women worked diligently, but it soon became obvious that we needed a full-time, paid editor. From 1976 to 1977, Linda Henry, a non-OA who had been our publications manager, became the *Lifeline* editor.

By this time the members of our office staff were being paid "real" salaries, and with the use of professional artists and beautiful cover photographs, our little bimonthly magazine took on a new look. When Linda resigned in April of 1977, OA's valiant volunteers came to the rescue again!

Finally, on July 11, 1977, our beloved Marianne E. joined the WSO staff as publications manager and *OA Lifeline* editor. She had an extensive background in publishing and editing, and for the next ten years under her expert guidance, our *Lifeline* became a monthly forum for OA news, stories, letters and discussions.

By this time my nineteen-year-old daughter, Julie, had become a graphic artist. Marianne welcomed her talents, and Julie served as a freelance designer and artist for *Lifeline* and other OA literature for several years.

After Marianne resigned in 1987, Carol H., Annette M. and then non-OA Michael Igoe came to WSO as *Lifeline* editors, while Sue P. served as our publications manager during the early 1990s. Subscriptions increased and there were more and more submissions from OA members in many countries.

In late 1994, when the World Service Office moved to Rio Rancho, New Mexico, just outside of Albuquerque, a whole new publications staff joined WSO. This was an exciting time for our expanding world services.

Non-OA members Sandra L. Herzog, publications manager, and Virginia Jensen, *OA Lifeline* editor, established a brand-new Publications Department. Both women had varied backgrounds in advertising, publishing, writing, editorial, graphic design and copy editing. They developed a handsome, professional look for our *Lifeline,* and the members responded enthusiastically.

Ever since our first mailing in 1962, the *Bulletin/Lifeline* had been our "meeting in print." Now, with input from all over the world and with improved format and graphic design, our little magazine promised to bring OA members many hours of encouragement and pleasure. It was truly our *Lifeline* between members!

Chapter Sixteen

I Put My Hand in Yours

E were offering an outstretched hand—OA's promise of hope and recovery. By early 1967, the need for newcomer and group help had become urgent.

Between 1960 and 1967, OA had exploded from just Jo and me in one meeting a week to one hundred groups across the United States.

Margaret, Hilda and Esther ran the General Service Office from their homes. Maxine managed our financial affairs, and Wendy was publishing our infant *OA Lifeline* from her home. I continued to write OA literature in my dining room. Group delegates and the seven-member Board of Trustees met annually to conduct our business affairs.

OA, however, was growing swiftly. New people wrote frantically for help and information; groups clamored for assistance with their problems. The situation was so chaotic that Margaret and I had a special meeting to search for solutions.

"Rozanne," she said, "it's my job to answer incoming letters, but I'm writing the same thing over and over." I reminded her that I had done the same thing when I was national secretary.

"I know," she went on. "I wish we could send an experienced member to every meeting to share answers to group problems and explain OA and our recovery program."

I'd been puzzling along those same lines for a long time,

and I thought I might have an answer. Handing her some papers, I said, "Take a look at this. I think we can send a handbook to serve as a stand-in for that experienced member you mentioned."

In 1961 I had written an eight-page booklet entitled *To Anyone Starting an Overeaters Anonymous Group* covering the basics of starting and running meetings as well as other facets of the OA program. Using that literature as a basis, I had begun to explore the best way to extend a helping hand to groups and members through the written word.

AA had always been a source of help to us, but because they were twenty-five years older than OA, their *Group Handbook* was too complicated for our needs.

What was the best approach for us? I envisioned myself and the older members physically reaching out to all those who came after us. As the idea took shape, that image became the theme of the new book.

The title of the book also came from that visual image— *I Put My Hand In Yours.*

As I wrote the first page, I closed my eyes and pictured myself reaching out to my OA sisters and brothers. It was as if I were talking to them, reassuring them with our collective experience, strength and hope.

In the book we offered suggestions based on our own experience, everything from setting up chairs to the importance of quiet and courtesy during the meeting. We discussed group officers, sponsorship, anonymity, money, literature and public attraction. We also described the *OA Lifeline*, our General Service Office, the annual Conference and the Board of Trustees. Many other details were covered, everything we could think of to help newcomers and groups in their search for stability and strength.

Although the main portion of the book was specific and practical, the opening page expressed our concern and love for struggling members and meetings everywhere:

> Remember, you are not alone. We are all with you all the time, even though you may feel lonely and far away from

other OA groups. . . . We in OA have suffered as you have, we have been helped by many powers outside of ourselves, and we have been shown a new way to live. We say in all sincerity, "Come with us and let us show you the way," and as we reach out to you, we truly hope that you will take heart and put your hand in ours.

First published in 1968, this book sported a bright red cover, which still catches the eye today. In 1989 the trustees asked me to write a "shell" around those first twenty-five pages, bringing the book up to date, yet preserving the precious original.

Although OA has since published a very helpful *Group Handbook* and related information, *I Put My Hand In Yours* offers a fascinating peek into how we handled ourselves when we were young and unsteadily growing.

That first paragraph of the original is OA's promise to compulsive overeaters everywhere:

I Put My Hand In Yours . . . and together we can do what we could never do alone! No longer is there a sense of hopelessness, no longer must we each depend upon our own unsteady willpower. We are all together now, reaching out our hands for power and strength greater than ours, and as we join hands, we find love and understanding beyond our wildest dreams.

Chapter Seventeen

The Language of the Heart

T was early 1979, the springtime of my Grand Adventure. During March and April I had been traveling across Europe alone, visiting friends in Greece and going to OA meetings in Rome and Naples.

Happily, Marvin joined me in Paris. Between our sight-seeing jaunts, I went to more meetings in that beautiful city. London was next, with new OA friends and welcoming fellowship.

I arrived back home in Los Angeles just in time to bring a report on the state of OA abroad to our 1979 annual World Service Conference.

Just picture this: It was the final hour of the Conference. I described the enormous difficulties overseas groups were having. Then I played a tape for the delegates which we'd made in Paris. It was European Maggie's poignant plea for help from America.

The effect on the assembly was electrifying! Steve H. from the San Fernando Valley jumped up in the back of the hall and declared, "I make a motion to establish a Conference International Committee with Rozanne as its chairperson." The delegates cheered and approved the motion unanimously, and for the first time in the history of OA, we had a Twelfth-Step structure devoted solely to the needs of members and groups outside the United States and Canada. The San Fernando Valley Intergroup voted to donate $300 to a special fund for "OA in Europe."

Chapter Seventeen

The next day I wrote a form letter which we sent to all overseas groups. This letter read in part:

THE LANGUAGE OF THE HEART

We care! Ich patlano! Vous nous êtes importante!
Endiaferómaste! Wïr kummern uns! Nos preoccupamos!

Whatever way we say it, we are all speaking the same language. We care about you . . . our OA sisters and brothers outside the United States!

Every day in thousands of meetings around the globe, words of hope, love and understanding are expressed between OA members. This is the true language of the heart.

It is in this spirit that a brand-new Conference Committee has been formed. . . . Its purpose is to provide supportive services to all of you—loners and groups—outside the United States. . . . The formation of the International Committee has sparked great enthusiasm here in the United States. American groups have volunteered to "adopt" an overseas group. Letters will be written, intergroup newsletters shared . . . and best of all, tapes of the weekly meetings here will be sent so that the struggling international groups will have a very specific idea of what the various OA meetings are like.

More information was included, and at the bottom of the letter we set up the same kind of return form we'd used on our response letters since the Paul Coates telecast.

OA groups in various locations had been organizing intergroups since the early 1970s. At the World Service Conference in 1976, the delegates had voted to establish eight OA regions in the United States. The regional trustees were elected in 1977, and in 1979 Myra K. was elected our first trustee-at-large for groups outside North America.

The following year the delegates became a functioning part of this committee. Since we'd all overlooked the fact that I wasn't a delegate, a new delegate chairman was elected. Then work began in earnest to carry the message to groups overseas. In 1981 the *International Newsletter* was established, and communication between groups around the world flourished.

In 1982 the position of trustee-at-large was abolished, and Region Nine trustee was established in its place. Region Nine was to service every place on planet Earth outside the United States and Canada. The election of Jeanine M. from Missouri as the new Region Nine trustee brought the number of our Board of Trustees to fifteen.

In 1988 Carol W. from Tel Aviv, Israel, was elected as our first overseas trustee. Building on Jeanine's splendid efforts, Carol worked diligently to carry the message to all corners of the globe, and OA continued to flourish everywhere.

Because of its rapid expansion, Region Nine became so unwieldy that many of its members began to talk about dividing the region into more manageable geographical areas. Discussions were carried on among the trustees and worldwide intergroups for several years.

One result of these talks was that Mexico was made part of Region Two in 1992. However, that was only a partial solution. Region Nine was still too big. What should be done?

Finally, after many sessions, the international delegates decided to divide into two sections, Region Nine and Region Ten. That meant that an amendment would have to be made to the Bylaws, with a motion for change submitted to the annual Conference.

The delegates involved were hesitant and fearful. "Will the North American delegates understand our decision and accept our request?" they asked one another. "Well," they agreed, "we just have to try."

Finally, the important day arrived. The motion for the establishment of Region Ten had been submitted to the 1994 World Service Business Conference under the appropriate sections of the OA Bylaws, Subpart B.

The meeting room was full; everyone was excited. When the time came to discuss the establishment of Region Ten, Carol G. from New York stood up. "I make a motion to accept the proposal by acclamation," she declared. Chairman David H. asked, "Does anybody object?" The delegates were silent, waiting. Not one person objected. "Then," said David, "the motion passes by acclamation!"

The entire room burst into applause and cheers. The Regions Nine and Ten delegates were crying and hugging one another, and there was literally dancing in the aisles!

As a result of this 1994 vote, Region Ten became comprised of countries and territories in the Far East, Southeast Asia, Australia, New Zealand and the Western Pacific Basin. All other non-North American groups remained in Region Nine.

That same year Hulda R. from Israel was elected Region Nine trustee. Carol W. was appointed Region Ten trustee until the next year's elections. In 1995 Violet L. from Australia was elected Region Ten trustee, bringing the number of trustees to sixteen.

I was overwhelmed and touched by all that had happened, and I knew that despite OA's long years of struggle, everything was worth the effort. Lives had been changed, relationships mended, friendships and partnerships born, bodies made healthy.

Above all, we were realizing at last that loving promise given on page 23 of *I Put My Hand In Yours*:

THE BOND OF BROTHERHOOD

In assuming responsibility, in sharing love and strength with one another, we create a bond between each of us. It can't be seen, but it can be felt in the heart—it's that bond of brotherhood between one overeater and another which clearly says: "I care, I put my hand in yours . . . now you are not alone."

A Thank-You Note

Gratitude is a such a small word to express the great depth of feeling we have for the many non-OA people who have supported and sustained us during all our growing-up years.

This is a thank you to:

Jim W.—the founder of Gamblers Anonymous. Your steady encouragement and wise guidance helped us establish a solid foundation for our Fellowship.

Paul Coates—Through your nationally-televised interview show, "Paul Coates' Confidential File," you were the first to publicize our original little meeting in late 1960.

Dear Abby—From that first letter you published in your newspaper column in 1965, as well as the public endorsement you've given us for many decades, you've directed thousands to a new way of life.

Ann Landers—Like your twin sister, Abby, you've let others know through your newspaper column that we offer a viable recovery program for compulsive overeaters.

Father Rollo M. Boas—As pastor of the Church of our Saviour in Los Angeles, you wrote a booklet about us and kept us focused when we seemed to stray from our purpose.

Marilyn Moore—As a nutrionist in the early 1970s, you not only guided us in creating a second eating plan, but you assisted our Fellowship by making your East Los Angeles Clinic rooms available for OA meetings.

Dr. Peter Lindner and Dr. William Rader—our friends in the medical profession who saw value in our program. You've publicly carried our message and sent many compulsive overeaters through our doors.

All our AA friends in Los Angeles—For our first ten years you spoke at our meetings week after week and led Twelve-Step study groups for us, teaching us about your recovery program and impressing upon us the importance of the Twelve Traditions—Chuck C., Nancy C., Dottie S., Marv R., Don R., Clancy I., Artie W., Jane B., Eddie C., Bobby E. and many other AAs in cities across the United States.

To every non-OA man and woman who has loved us, encouraged us and believed in us over the years, we offer our heartfelt appreciation.